Sweet Dreams

Sweet Dreams

A Pediatrician's Secrets for Your Child's Good Night's Sleep

Paul M. Fleiss, M.D., M.P.H.
with Frederick M. Hodges, D. Phil.

LOWELL HOUSE

LOS ANGELES

NTC/Contemporary Publishing Group

The purpose of this book is to educate. It is sold with the understanding that the publisher and author shall have neither liability nor responsibility for any injury caused or alleged to be caused directly or indirectly by the information contained in this book. While every effort has been made to ensure its accuracy, the book's contents should not be construed as medical advice. Each person's health needs are unique. To obtain recommendations appropriate to your particular situation, please consult a qualified health care provider.

Library of Congress Cataloging-in-Publication Data

Fleiss, Paul.
    Sweet dreams : a pediatrician's secrets for your child's good night's sleep / Paul M. Fleiss, with Frederick M. Hodges.
       p.   cm.
    Includes bibliographical references and index.
    ISBN 0-7373-0494-4 (paperback)
    1. Sleep disorders in children—Popular works.   2. Children—Sleep.   I. Hodges, Frederick Mansfield.   II. Title.

RJ506.S55 F54   2000
618.92'8498—dc21   00-064149
                                                                   CIP

Published by Lowell House
A division of NTC/Contemporary Publishing Group, Inc.
4255 West Touhy Avenue, Lincolnwood, Illinois 60712 U.S.A.

Managing Director and Publisher: Jack Artenstein
Executive Editor: Peter Hoffman
Director of Publishing Services: Rena Copperman
Managing Editor: Jama Carter
Editor: Claudia McCowan
Project Editor: Carmela Carvajal

Design by Susan H. Hartman

Printed in the United States of America
International Standard Book Number: 0-7373-0494-4
    01 02 03 04 DHD 18 17 16 15 14 13 12 11 10 9 8 7 6 5 4 3 2

Don't Let the Baby Cry

Don't let the baby cry
She only wants to love you.

Don't let the baby cry
He only wants to see you.

Don't let the baby cry
She only wants to touch you.

Don't let the baby cry
He only wants to hear you.

Don't let the baby cry
She only wants to savour you.

Don't let the baby cry
He only wants to feel you.

Don't let the baby cry
She only wants to know you.

Don't let the baby cry
He only wants to love you.

—Laura Huxley
FOUNDER AND PRESIDENT OF
CHILDREN: OUR ULTIMATE INVESTMENT

Contents

Introduction

$\int$leep, even after countless centuries of observation, remains a
mystery, and the results of our most laborious studies and our
most painstaking research only emphasize this fact. In recent decades,
however, innovative scientific investigation has raised the veil slightly and
given us a glimpse into the fascinating truths about sleep. One great fact
that has emerged recently is that sleep is a dynamic, positive, vital, constructive, and active process. It is not a cessation of activity, but an ampli-
fication of a wide range of vital functions. It is the positive, constructive
character of sleep that explains why babies, who are at the period of their
most rapid growth and development, sleep from sixteen to eighteen hours
a day. This marvelous capacity for sleep and rapid development steadily
diminishes until adult life is reached, at which point it becomes constant,
in the neighborhood of nine hours.

The most fundamental question about sleep that everyone asks is:
"How much sleep should I get?" This can be answered unhesitatingly in
five short words: "As much as you can." Consequently, the goal of parents
these days should be to create an environment in which they and their

children can obtain as much sleep as possible. After all, it is during sleep that the body refreshes, repairs, and rejuvenates itself. To limit this beneficial process is to risk diminishing life, health, and happiness. This book, then, is addressed to those parents who desire to help their children get the rich and satisfying sleep that everyone requires and to help them avoid or solve common sleep problems.

Naturally, all good parents want this for themselves as well as for their children. Ironically, though, Americans are experiencing more sleep problems than ever before. It is natural, then, that the number of reports of children's sleep problems has risen in recent years. As a result of this heightened concern, the study of child sleep has become of major interest to scientists. Entire medical conferences are organized around the fascinating subject of sleep. There now exist several medical journals that publish nothing but studies relating to sleep. Even general medical journals regularly publish the latest scientific data on child sleep. Predictably, much of this new information works its way into newspaper reports. Unfortunately, many of these reports can sometimes be confusing or contradictory. Parents are often left with more questions and doubts than they had before.

As to be expected, there are many controversies about sleep. Parents want to know, for instance, whether it is safe to share a bed with their babies and young children. Parents have heard contradictory views on this and many other subjects, but where can they turn for accurate, unbiased information so that they can make an informed choice that is right for their family?

I have written this book to provide parents with the latest and most accurate information on sleep—the very information that parents want and need. In addition to a detailed and thoroughly researched presentation on bed-sharing, this book addresses all of the major sleep controversies that concern parents today. For instance, I address the controversies over strict feeding schedules, firm bedtimes, and "crying it out" methods. I am confident that this solidly scientific approach will enable you to be a better and more informed parent—one who will be more comfortable trusting the traditional wisdom that love, gentle and informed guidance, physical affection, compassion, sympathy, and generosity are the parental gifts that achieve the greatest results and make for the most productive, happiest, healthiest, steadiest, and most well-rested children.

One feature of this book about which I am very proud is that it is based on a well-documented and rigorous review of the latest scientific literature. I have provided the supporting references from the medical literature so that parents can learn more about the issues that interest them. The superscripted numbers at the end of phrases and sentences refer to the corresponding scientific citations that will be found at the end of the book. Few childcare books make this commitment to scientific honesty, but I think they should. Parents who would like additional information on any of the subjects mentioned in the book can then easily identify and locate the scientific studies that I consulted. This helpful feature will give parents access to the accurate and unbiased scientific information they will need to help their children enjoy beautiful, restful sleep.

Parents who read this book will learn that fostering good sleep patterns in their children can be easily achieved, but it requires a long-term commitment. Parents need to adopt a holistic approach that takes into account every aspect of a child's existence. It means deeply involving yourself in your child's life. It requires establishing and maintaining a deep bond of love, compassion, and generosity with your children. The good news is that the benefits of that bond are much greater than a good night's sleep.

The foundations of your child's sleep patterns are set in the morning and maintained throughout the day. Therefore, in this book, I show parents in a step-by-step way how they can successfully steer their child throughout the day in the direction of healthy sleep patterns. Human sleep patterns change throughout our lives. A newborn infant, for instance, sleeps in a remarkably different way from a toddler or a child. A child sleeps in an entirely different way from an adult. Each age group has its own unique sleeping pattern. It is part of our growth and development as human beings. Recognizing and appreciating the developmental stages of sleep will help parents avoid holding unrealistic expectations.

One of the primary messages of this book is that because each child is unique, you are the only one who can adapt the recommendations in this book to fit the personality, temperament, and tastes of your child. By committing yourself to loving involvement and interaction with your child, you will discover what works best. Using the guidelines offered, you will be able to foster a healthy and enjoyable sleep routine for your child. If you have more than one child, you may find that what works for one will be less successful with another. It is only by dedicating yourself to a full commitment to each of your children that you will discover the right approach for each child. Your experience as a parent will be infinitely richer and more deeply rewarding as a result. You will be establishing a lasting bond of love and respect that will sustain the relationship between you and your child for the rest of your lives.

Another vitally important message of this book is that many of the so-called "sleep problems" that parents report in their children are actually the result of unreasonable expectations, usually based on unrealistic myths about how children are supposed to be. New parents are often unable to determine the accuracy of the advice they receive from well-meaning grandparents, neighbors, friends, or childcare books. With the best of intentions, parents are sometimes induced to follow bad advice. Babies, however, cannot be tricked by unreasonable expectations. The baby's inability to adjust to "feeding schedules" and rigid "sleep training" indicates that these expectations are unnatural and incapable of meeting the baby's biological needs. By presenting parents with the most up-to-date and accurate scientific facts, combined with the invaluable experience I have gained over several decades as a pediatrician, this book shatters these myths and presents the fascinating facts of child sleep. Not only will these facts help you to understand your child's natural, biological sleep patterns, but they will help you understand and better appreciate your child.

Prepare yourself to deepen your involvement in your baby's development. Watch your baby grow and learn. Cherish every moment of your baby's exciting new adventure on earth. There is nothing you will ever do that is as rewarding, meaningful, enriching, interesting, fascinating, or memorable as lovingly raising a child. There is no play as dramatic, no game as thrilling, and no meal as satisfying as observing and participating in your baby's development. The growth and development of a human being is the most amazing adventure there is.

With a little bit of learning, we can free ourselves from the old myths of our parents' and grandparents' generations and instead act upon our native intuition, instinct, intelligence, generosity, selflessness, love, and compassion to help our children grow up to be the healthiest, strongest, smartest, happiest, and most caring humans possible. Fostering good sleep patterns in our children is only part of that mission, but it is also one of the most important.

Chapter 1

What Is Sleep?

*S*leep is a dynamic, fascinating, and mysterious process. Although modern science still has not discovered all of the reasons why we need to sleep, we do know for a fact that a good night's sleep is more than just the *result* of good health—it is the *foundation* of good health. This is as true for you as it is for your child. Sleep is not only vital for humans, it is vital for all animal life on earth. Even the lowliest worms and insects sleep. It is a universal function that all animal life shares in common.

It is comforting to know, however, that it is unnecessary for science to tell us why we need to sleep in order to help us persuade our children to sleep. Children rarely need to be convinced of its importance in order to engage in it. It is so natural that there is little we can do to prevent children from falling asleep when they are drowsy, except under the most extraordinarily stressful circumstances and, even then, not for long.

Most parents assume that the purpose of sleep is to rest the body. Parents lovingly observe the peaceful nighttime sleep of their children and mark the contrast between this state of tranquillity and repose with their child's daytime whirlwind of energetic activity. Certainly, your child's body does rest during sleep, and we all know that rest is beneficial, but actually, during sleep, very little of the body actually rests. Your child's body is really quite active during sleep. The internal organs continue to function. The heart never stops pumping. The diaphragm never stops repeating its rhythmic, alternating pattern of contraction and relaxation. The digestion slows but continues nonetheless. The most we can say is that, during sleep, some of your child's many bodily systems continue their activity, but at a more relaxed tempo. The endocrine system, however, seems to be most active during sleep. This is the system of chemical messengers—hormones—that regulates your child's bodily functions.

Many parents also assume that sleep serves the purpose of resting the brain. We can say with confidence, however, that the brains of young and old do not become inactive during sleep. In fact, during some phases of sleep, the brain is even more active than when we are awake. Nonetheless, sleep does give our brains a break from the waking world, a break that seems to be beneficial to our mind and body.

We tend to forget that our brain is a complex electrochemical powerhouse. Every normal activity seems to be tied to an internal chemical reaction. Sleep is one of those activities whose every phase is mirrored by chemical activities. For instance, sleep has important effects on brain and tissue glucose utilization,[1] which is a fancy way of saying that sleep itself regulates how our body manages its energy supply. This is an important clue to parents of school-age children that a good night's sleep plays a crucial role in preparing your child for a productive and rewarding school day.

Sometimes, we imagine that hormones are just related to puberty, but from conception throughout the entire span of life, our hormones regulate our bodily functions, growth, repair, and development. It is convenient, therefore, to think of the daily release of hormones into our bloodstream as the key force behind our biological rhythms. Without sleep, or without adequate or restful sleep, our biological rhythms become disrupted, and ill health follows.

One of the important hormones that I will mention several times throughout this book is cortisol. Among other things, this hormone regulates the release of stored energy and prepares our body and mind for the next day's activities. Just before we wake up, it reaches its highest level of concentration in our bloodstream. Additionally, in both boys and girls, free cortisol levels increase by 50 to 75 percent within the first thirty minutes after waking.[2] This rise in cortisol, however, which helps your child wake up in the morning and maintain an even energy level throughout the day, can be disrupted by stress.[3] As I shall point out in subsequent chapters, eliminating avoidable causes of short-term or even chronic stress from your child's life is vitally important if you want your child to be at the peak of his performance abilities, both asleep and awake.

Under the best of circumstances, we are unaware of the tide of cortisol and the other hormones that wash through us during the day and during sleep. We do not have any consciousness of their individual existences or the roles they play in our health or in our sense of well-being. All we know is that we have risen from our beds awake, refreshed, full of energy, vitality, and good cheer.

Sleep Patterns Throughout Life

One of the most important messages that science has delivered to us about sleep is that we experience different sleep patterns at every stage of our life. This is not a matter of habit, convention, or will. It is regulated by our evolving neurochemistry and our biological clock. As we move through life, there is a parallel evolution in the amount of sleep we need to feel refreshed again, and an evolution in the time(s) of day that we sleep. The proportion of sleep time spent dreaming also steadily changes throughout life. Additionally, given the important links between sleep phases, brain wave patterns, and hormone release into the bloodstream, we should not be surprised to learn that the differences in the sleep patterns of humans at various stages of life are mirrored by differences in hormone secretions. This information is vitally important for parents because it will banish unrealistic expectations. The information on sleep patterns will also give parents a rough time line of the changes in sleep patterns that they can expect to observe in their children.

As I will explain in greater detail later in this chapter, science has discovered that there are seven levels in the sleep/wakefulness cycle, ranging from fully awake to deeply asleep. One of the most interesting stages is *rapid eye movement sleep* (REM sleep). During this stage, the eyes rapidly move back and forth, as if they were following the action in a busy street scene. In fact, it is during REM sleep that we dream, and so it might be useful to imagine that the movement of our physical eyes may parallel the movement of our dream eyes. Because dreaming is so fascinating, it is convenient to divide sleep phases into REM sleep and non-REM sleep.

In order to understand their children's "sleep problems," it is vital that parents learn to distinguish genuine sleep problems from unrealistic expectations. When we understand that infants, children, teenagers, adults, and the elderly all have unique sleep patterns, we will gain more respect for our children and their unique biological state. This understanding will help us to become better parents. Ignoring the natural biological rhythms and sleep patterns of our children can only lead to frustration.

To put it in the simplest of terms, a newborn baby sleeps differently than a four-month-old baby. A four-month-old baby exhibits a sleep pattern that is different from that of a toddler. A toddler has a sleep cycle that differs from that of a ten-year-old child. A ten-year-old child, in turn, has a sleep pattern distinct from that of a teenager, whose sleep pattern is different from that of an adult, and from that of a grandparent, whose sleep pattern is more different still. We should not expect our babies to sleep the way we sleep or even to sleep the way the neighbors' children of the same age sleep. Every person is unique and special, and we should adjust our expectations to whatever the individual pattern happens to be. We should free ourselves from the unhealthy expectation that we can or should "condition" our babies to behave as we want them to, as if they were dogs that we train to sit on command.

Sleep in the Fetus

Most parents are surprised to learn that the unborn baby experiences periods of sleep and wakefulness. The fetus spends from sixteen to twenty hours a day sleeping. In fact, most of the kicking that a fetus engages in actually takes place while she is asleep. Of special interest, researchers have discovered that during REM sleep, a male fetus experiences penile erection.[4] In the same study, researchers also found that the male fetus even experiences erections about 16 percent of the time during non-REM sleep. Additionally, the fetus is unique in that he spends 60 to 80 percent of his sleep time in REM sleep.

Although, for obvious reasons, the fetus cannot perceive sunlight, she has already developed daily sleep cycles. The sunlight-regulated hormones that set the mother's internal clock are transmitted through the placenta. Thus, through this chemical language, a mother prepares her unborn baby for life outside the womb.

Sleep in Babies

The newborn baby spends 75 percent of his time asleep. This is because a baby's physiological sleep need is vastly different from that of an adult. Babies are also unique in that they spend 50 percent of their daily sleep in REM sleep. Just after birth, babies only seem to have two stages of sleep: REM sleep and non-REM sleep. Unlike adults, babies often move during REM sleep and remain still during non-REM sleep. For this reason, REM sleep at this stage of life is sometimes called "active sleep," and non-REM sleep is often called "quiet sleep."

Unfortunately, many parents have been led to believe·that a baby can and should sleep like an adult. Still others have been told that they can "train" their baby to sleep like an adult. Neither of these two ideas is correct. Babies are unique in their physiological needs and patterns. Babies are not adults, and there is nothing you can do to turn them into adults overnight. The transition from babyhood to adulthood takes eighteen or more years. Let your baby be a baby, and both you and your baby will be much happier.

As your baby grows, her sleep patterns evolve and become more like those of older children, but just because your baby reaches four months of age and some "expert" says that she no longer needs to awaken for a night feeding does not mean that your baby does not need *you* when she awakens in the middle of the night. A human baby has more needs than merely the need to be fed. He does not wake up simply to annoy you and deprive you of a good night's sleep. A baby's physiology, vastly different from that of an adult or even an older child, means that he simply cannot adopt an adult's sleeping schedule. A newborn baby, for instance, has an almost continuous need for feeding and holding. An adult, by contrast, has developed beyond the need for continuous feeding and can thrive on three regularly spaced meals a day and one eight-hour period of sleep at nighttime.

Naturally, sleep-starved parents would like nothing more than for babies to adopt adult sleep patterns immediately after birth, but this, I am afraid, is impossible. Being the parent of a newborn child necessarily means incurring a sleep deficit for a few months. There is good news, however. As the adult, you have the power to be flexible. For instance, you can win yourself some valuable sleep time by learning to sleep when the baby sleeps. After all, the newborn will have a total of sixteen to twenty hours of sleep in a twenty-four-hour day. You may be able to create a schedule that will allow you to get your eight hours of sleep somewhere within the many periods that your baby is asleep. Of course, you can look forward to the time when your baby will reach the stage of growth and development when she will want to spend less of her daytime asleep, and more time exploring her environment, learning what her body and mind can do.

Not surprisingly, a baby's sleep patterns are matched by unique biological markers. At three months of age, babies develop a twenty-four-hour sleep/wakefulness cycle that parallels the development of the daily pattern in adrenocortical brain activity.[5] This does not mean, however, that babies will then sleep like adults. The older the baby gets, the stronger the early morning peak in the levels of the hormone cortisol. Once the rhythm of the surges of cortisol begins to mimic the pattern seen in adult biological rhythms, babies will usually begin to sleep through the night.[6] Yet, even after that, a baby's sleep patterns still do not resemble those of an adult. Your baby will merely have moved to the next stage of sleep evolution. I am afraid that there is nothing you can do to speed up this process. Just enjoy your baby for who he is. Babies do not *start* to sleep through the night in earnest until well after the third month of life, and, even then, they may wake up periodically for comforting. Babies may sleep through some nights but awaken periodically other nights. Only after about six months do most babies sleep through most nights. There is much variation in this development, so do not worry if your baby takes a longer or shorter amount of time to reach this stage.

Sleep in Children

By about two years of age, children will sleep approximately half of a twenty-four-hour period. This feat is accomplished by naps in the morning and in the afternoon, in addition to nighttime sleep periods. Thereafter, they slowly graduate to a pattern of sleeping in ten-hour stretches during the night without sleeping during the day. This pattern generally holds until puberty. Because they get so much sleep, children are usually filled with energy during the day. They are bright and exuberant. In children, sleep is marked by an increase in hormonal activity. For instance, in both boys and girls, sleep is connected with a significant rise in prolactin levels. This process occurs very early in childhood, including children as young as one year.[7]

Prolactin is a peptide hormone secreted by the lactotroph of the anterior pituitary gland in the brain. It is essential for the production of milk in nursing mothers, but it is also released in large quantities into the bloodstream of males, non-nursing adult females, and children. Prolactin secretion is induced by sleep, stress, sexual activity, and, in women, the suckling stimulus. Someday we may better understand the many roles that this interesting hormone plays. Even though the brains of both males and females produce prolactin, there remain various gender-based differences in the activity of prolactin during sleep.[8]

In normal, well-nourished children, the primary "sleep problem" seems to be a reluctance to go to bed. Although this is not a genuine medical problem, parents usually consider it as such because it can vex them. When children get tired, they can become cranky, less attentive, and careless. At the same time, they can become more active. Nervous energy propels them to new heights of frenzied activity. Ironically, most children in this state vehemently deny that they are tired. Usually, however, resistance to bedtime is not the child's fault. Instead, I think it is usually due to a parent's failure to establish positive bedtime rituals. (See chap. 6.)

Sleep in Teenagers

When it comes to sleep, teenagers are the most maligned group there is. They are alternately accused of getting too much sleep—especially on weekend mornings—and of getting too little sleep—especially on weekend evenings. One of the most fascinating discoveries about the teenage years is that the miraculous changes that occur during puberty occur during sleep. Additionally, the pattern of sleep changes quite dramatically during the teenage years. For instance, between the ages of ten and twelve, the amount of sleep that children get each night reduces to an average of about 9.33 hours. Also, four years immediately after the onset of puberty, teenagers make the transition to a truly adult sleep pattern.[9] Among other things, this means that your child will not start to share your adult sleeping patterns until he reaches the age of sixteen or so.

In the first two years of puberty, teenagers experience an average of 2.5 awakenings each night, whereas teenagers in the last two years of puberty experience an average of only 1.2 awakenings each night. Puberty also sees a sharp decrease in the number of REM sleep periods. If children enjoy an average of 6.9 periods of REM sleep each night, adolescents experience only 4 per night. This number remains constant through young adulthood.

Research shows that sleep is critically important for growth and maturation during the teenage years. The hormones that regulate these processes are secreted in significantly increased amounts into the bloodstream during sleep, rather than during the day. One can conclude, then, that without adequate sleep, growth may be stunted.

Parents often joke that teenagers are governed by their hormones rather than their intellects. It certainly is true that the hormone surges of puberty can affect a teenager's moods and perceptions, but these same hormone surges are also intimately related to sleep. Important hormones such as testosterone, follicle-stimulating hormone, and luteinizing hormone are all produced in much larger amounts and released during sleep in both boys and girls. These are not the only hormones that increase production. In teenage boys, a sleep-associated rise in prolactin levels occurs at all stages of puberty.[10] Indeed, studies confirm the fascinating fact that the release of prolactin in adolescent boys is linked with sleep itself—whenever it occurs—rather than with clock time.[11] As we might expect, the peaks of prolactin release appear clearly during cycles of REM sleep. For prepubescent boys, the average number of night peaks of prolactin is higher than that in boys who are past puberty.[12]

Additionally, the secretion of luteinizing hormone—a sex hormone that plays a critical role in sexual maturation of both boys and girls—takes on an adult pattern and increases dramatically during Stage IV, non-REM sleep. This pattern is also seen in adult males.[13] Puberty is also the time during which testosterone secretion takes on the same pattern that will be maintained in young adulthood: Testosterone secretion levels begin to rise on falling asleep, peak at about the time of first REM, and remain at the same levels until awakening.[14]

Among the many other hormones whose secretion and timing evolve during puberty, melatonin undergoes changes in its rhythm. Melatonin seems to play a key role in signaling the onset of puberty. It is the systematic decrease in evening melatonin levels that instructs the body to begin the process of sexual maturation.

Growth hormone is a powerful anabolic hormone that affects all bodily systems and plays an important role in muscle growth. Like many other hormones that are important in sleep, it is released from the anterior pituitary in response to a variety of stimuli, which include exercise, sleep, and even stress. In addition to being responsible for a dramatic effect on longitudinal growth, growth hormone is now known to exert generalized effects on protein, lipid, and carbohydrate metabolism. There is also some indication that growth hormone may be involved in the regulation of immune function, mental well-being, and the aging process.[15] Growth hormone is present in normal and healthy persons of both sexes from early childhood until late adulthood.

Because of the critical role that sleep plays during puberty, we should not be surprised that teenagers actually require as much if not more sleep than children half their age. Unfortunately, the increased sleep need of teenagers has rarely been understood as the biologically controlled, physiological need that it is. Instead, it has traditionally been mistaken as a sign that teenagers are "lazy" and "uncooperative." If teenagers do not meet their sleep requirement, their growth may suffer, and, at the very least, they will suffer from drowsiness and impaired functioning during the day.[16] These are not the only consequences of the chronic pattern of sleep deficiency in teenagers. Other consequences include vulnerability to catastrophic accidents, mood and behavior problems, increased vulnerability to drugs and alcohol, and development of major disorders of the sleep/wakefulness cycle.[17]

One of the problems facing most American teenagers is that the early waking hour imposed on them during the school term obliges them to sacrifice their biological sleep needs. To make matters worse, homework and social demands prevent teenagers from going to bed as early as they should, given their schedule of early rising. Thus, early school start time is associated with disruptions in normal REM and slow-wave sleep patterns, significant sleep deprivation, and daytime sleepiness.[18] Clearly, for the health of our children and the peace of mind of parents, it would be best if our society could find a way to start school later in the day for teenagers, and if teenagers would readjust their social priorities.

Sleep in Adults

In adulthood, our need for sleep gradually decreases. Adults simply do not need as much sleep as children, and certainly not as much as teenagers. If teenagers require 10 to 12 hours of sleep per night, the number of hours adults need to sleep each night reduces, on average, to 7.06 hours.[19] Middle-age adults only require about 7 hours of sleep. Additionally, adults spend only 25 percent of their sleep time in REM sleep, which represents only about 2 hours a night.

Similarly, the amount of slow-wave sleep decreases dramatically over the same narrow age range.[20] Adult sleep patterns are unique, but, even then, they only last a few decades before evolving into something completely different.

Sleep in the Elderly

In the elderly, there is a decline in sleep continuity, a decrease in slow-wave sleep, an earlier nocturnal cortisol rise, and a gradual blunting of growth hormone secretion.[21] The elderly also experience significantly reduced nocturnal awakenings and an increased first non-REM sleep period. Similarly, the elderly enjoy the least amount of REM sleep of all the age groups, experiencing the REM stage only about 15 to 20 percent of their sleep time. In contrast to men in younger age groups, the majority of men older than sixty do not have full sleep erections.[22] Also, the amount of time spent in Stage III and Stage IV sleep gradually decreases to almost nothing.

In old age, sleep is more susceptible to internal arousing stimuli associated with misalignment of the internal clock.[23] The propensity to awaken from sleep advances relative to the decrease in body temperature in older people. As part of the breakdown of regular sleep patterns, elderly people tend to fall asleep frequently during the day and wake up frequently during the night.

The Internal Clock

Our daily sleep patterns are tied to the circadian pacemaker, which is located in a deep structure in the human brain, called the suprachiasmatic nucleus of the hypothalamus. It functions as our internal clock and is a very delicate structure that is easily influenced by our behaviors, activities, and habits.

The intrinsic period of the internal clock averages 24.18 hours,[24] which is almost identical to the length of one Earth day. Its rhythms regulate many physiologic and hormonal functions whose daily oscillations, in turn, govern the release of nearly every hormone. This is just as true for infants as it is for grandparents.

The internal clock, however, does not control sleep. Instead, it controls wakefulness. Sleep itself plays a powerful role in maintaining, regulating, setting, and adjusting our internal clock. In other words, the same internal clock that awakens us from sleep can be altered by our sleep habits.

You may ask, then, what controls sleep? Sleep seems to be under the control of a homeostatic process in the brain that normally functions in partnership with the internal clock. The internal clock, which is set by our exposure to daylight, in turn regulates the timing and pattern of sleep by generating a rhythm of sleep propensity.[25] Not surprisingly, propensity for sleep increases at the end of the day. This coincides with the onset of melatonin secretion, which normally takes place between nine and ten o'clock in the evening.

As you will find, much of the advice that I give in this book is aimed at properly setting and resetting your child's internal clock. Whether your child is a newborn or a teenager, a good night's sleep depends on the proper alignment of the internal clock with the rotation of the earth. You will be surprised to learn how easy it is to disrupt the internal clock and thereby disrupt sleep.

Stages of Sleep

As I have already mentioned, it is very helpful for parents to know that sleep researchers have discovered that there are seven levels in the sleep/wakefulness cycle (see Table 1), all characterized by a unique type of brain wave, which is measured by a device called an electroencephalograph (EEG). A complete run through these levels is called a *sleep cycle*. Our brain smoothly progresses from one level to the next throughout the night. Within these levels, there are two levels of wakefulness, four stages of sleep, and, finally, a special level of sleep characterized by rapid eye movement (REM). Like so many things in life, the amount of time we spend in any one of the stages of sleep depends on our age.

One of the few features of sleep common to all age groups is that midway through the night, our body temperature drops, usually two full

Table 1

Levels of the Sleep/Wakefulness Cycle

Level	Description	Brain Wave Pattern
Level I	Wakefulness	Beta waves
Level 2	Relaxed wakefulness	Alpha waves
Stage I sleep	Mild unconsciousness	Theta waves
Stage II sleep	Deeper unconsciousness	Sleep spindles and K-complexes
Stage III sleep	Deep sleep	Delta waves and theta waves
Stage IV sleep	Slow-wave deep sleep	Delta waves
Rapid eye movement (REM) sleep	Dream state	Theta, alpha, and beta waves

degrees below our normal daytime temperature. It is very interesting to note that this drop in body temperature is constant across the transition from one stage of sleep to the next.

The first level in the sleep/wakefulness cycle is not really a level of sleep at all, but the condition of wakefulness that we usually experience throughout the day when we are wide awake. Newborn babies spend the least amount of time in the first level, for the obvious reason that they spend so much of their time asleep. The more we age, the more time we spend awake. Only in advanced age do we begin to experience a decrease in the amount of time spent awake.

The type of brain wave at this stage is a low-voltage type called a beta wave. Still, parents of children of all ages will notice that their child's state of wakefulness is altered slightly when the child starts to get tired at the end of the day. About an hour before your child's usual bedtime, his body temperature begins to drop. He relaxes and becomes calm. The pineal gland in your child's brain starts releasing the hormone melatonin into his bloodstream. As I have pointed out, the cycle of melatonin release is not influenced by sleep but is dependent on exposure to light and darkness. It also has the effect of preparing us physically and mentally for sleep. This is as true for you as it is for your child, whatever his age.

Once your child lies down in bed and closes his eyes, he enters the next level of sleep. Here, your child's brain makes the transition from beta wave to alpha wave, which is a slower wave of higher strength. During this level of calm wakefulness, your child's mind wanders, and he is deeply relaxed.

Next, your child enters the first stage of real sleep. The brain wave characterized by Stage I sleep is the theta wave, which is of an even lower frequency than the alpha wave. In this stage, your child enters a mild state of unconsciousness. His brain ignores the sounds, sights, smells, tastes, and textures of the outside world. Also during Stage I sleep, your child's eyes will begin to roll slowly back and forth. Although Stage I sleep is true sleep, it is a light sleep. We can easily be awakened at this stage. In fact, if we are awakened from Stage I sleep, we do not have the perception of having been asleep at all.

You may have noticed that when you read a bedtime story to your child, he may close his eyes and appear to be asleep and deeply relaxed. Yet, the moment you think that you can safely stop reading, close the book, and tiptoe out of the room, he will perk up, insist that he was not asleep, and implore you to finish the story. Despite his protestations, your child most likely had entered Stage I sleep when his eyes were closed. Even so, during Stage I sleep, your child's brain remains vigilant for signs of change in the environment.

Under normal circumstances, we remain in Stage I sleep for about five minutes before making the descent into Stage II sleep. Here, the brain produces two very peculiar types of waves called sleep spindles and K-complexes. Each of these waves lasts only about two seconds, the pattern repeating for about ten minutes.

Following Stage II sleep, we make the transition to Stage III sleep, which is the first level of deep sleep. If you observe your child when he is at this stage, you will notice that his breathing is very shallow, his limbs are loose and relaxed, and he looks utterly peaceful and content. Here, the brain produces delta waves, which are large, regular, and of lower frequency than theta waves. In addition to the delta wave, the brain continues to produce tiny bursts of theta waves, sleep spindles, and K-complexes, but the rolling delta wave soon predominates. In Stage III sleep, the brain erects a firm barrier between the outside world and our internal consciousness. When your child progresses to Stage III sleep, it is very difficult to awaken him.

Stage III sleep lasts only a short while before it evolves into Stage IV sleep—the stage of true slow-wave deep sleep. For this reason, it is also called slow-wave sleep. Here, the brain produces only the slow delta wave. At this stage, it is difficult to be awakened. Just as in Stage III sleep, in Stage IV, you will notice that your child's muscles are deeply relaxed and his heart and breathing decrease their tempo. In children as well as in adults, Stage IV sleep is also characterized by the release of specialized hormones into the bloodstream. The results of many studies highlight the complexity of hormone and sleep interactions.[26] Among the many hormones released at this time, the brain releases growth hormone as well as prolactin. One of the differences between the sleep patterns of adults and children is that children spend a significantly greater amount of time in Stage IV sleep before moving on to the next stage. This makes perfect sense because children, especially babies, are in a period of rapid growth and development. What is surprising to most parents is that growth takes place during sleep.

After Stage IV sleep, we return to Stage III sleep for about ten minutes, but we are not on the road to wakefulness. Instead, we enter into the deepest and most mysterious level of sleep, the dream state, otherwise known as REM sleep. Here, the eyes move rapidly back and forth under the eyelids. The brain increases its activity, while the muscles of the body become completely relaxed. While we dream, we are conscious, but we are conscious in a different reality—a reality of our own creation. In REM sleep, our brain no longer produces delta waves but alternates between theta waves, alpha waves, and beta waves. Our brain is just as alive and active as when we are awake. Experiencing the right amount of REM sleep each night is important for adequate information processing in the brain, especially concerning memory functions and learning processes.

In healthy males, another remarkable feature of REM sleep is penile erection. Nocturnal penile erections are present throughout the life of the healthy male, with only a slight decline in older healthy males.[27,28] Additionally, as we saw above, the fetus experiences erections during REM sleep. As one might expect, they are most frequent and most vigorous in boys experiencing the changes of puberty.[29] It is not yet clear to science, however, what function erections serve during REM sleep. Obviously, they are important and necessary, for otherwise they would not occur. Nocturnal penile erections, then, are a sign of good health and vitality and mean that your son is getting a good night's sleep. One thing we do know is that testosterone levels increase during REM sleep with erection.[30] Testosterone itself plays a relatively specific and discrete role in regulating sleep and daily biological rhythms.[31] (Analogous phenomena are present in females during REM sleep, the most striking of which is uterine contraction.[32]) Interestingly, in healthy males of all ages, dreams are almost always accompanied by nocturnal penile erection. These erections are unrelated to dream content, for they are present during both erotic and nonerotic dreams.

Many children, and many adults as well, do not remember their dreams. This may lead them to conclude that they do not dream. Whether or not dreams are recalled, it is safe to assume that the vast majority of unmedicated healthy people dream during the night. If you notice that your sleeping child's eyes are moving rapidly underneath her eyelids, it is a safe bet that she is in REM sleep and that she is dreaming. Usually, we experience our final period of REM sleep just before waking up. It is usually the dreams experienced during this final period that we remember most vividly.

During the night, after your child goes to bed, the first period of REM sleep he will experience will usually last only about ten minutes. This first episode of dreaming is soon followed by the dreamless and calmer levels of deep sleep—Stages III and IV. Throughout the night, your child will normally experience five or six complete sleep cycles, moving from deep sleep to brief, unremembered periods of wakefulness and then back again. Consequently, he will experience five or six periods of dream-filled REM sleep.

Sleep is a biological phenomenon of enormous complexity, and my descriptions above convey only a small fraction of the fascinating information that science is discovering about sleep. I hope that you have gained an appreciation for the miracle of sleep and for the evolution of sleep patterns and phases that takes place over a lifetime. I also hope that you will look at your children with new eyes and renewed respect.

Rest may be one of the benefits of sleep, but, as we have seen, some of the body's most important processes occur only during sleep. Without engaging in the sleep process, our bodies would not mature, and we would be unable to function properly. For each stage of human development, there is a corresponding pattern of sleep. Development and sleep are inextricably intertwined.

Naturally, recognizing that different age groups have unique sleep patterns and sleep needs will help us to be better parents. Once we have this information, we will no longer cling to the old-fashioned and uninformed notion that everyone should be expected to adopt adult sleep patterns on command. After all, you too are only passing through a transitory and temporary pattern of sleep. Whatever your age, your present sleep pattern will eventually evolve and change. Trying to force your baby to evolve prematurely into the next sleep pattern is as futile as commanding your baby to go through puberty immediately. Life does not work this way.

Learn to treasure your child—whatever her age—for the unique being that she is. Accept her for who she is, and do not make your own life unpleasant by expecting your child to exhibit behaviors that her current stage of biological development will not allow her to display.

We cannot *fight* Mother Nature, but we can *work* with Mother Nature to help our children get the best night's sleep possible. The rest of this book is dedicated to helping you discover simple ways of making your child's sleep time more rewarding.

Chapter 2

How to Handle Night Wakings and Other Sleep Problems

*A*t various stages of childhood, children may wake up in the middle of the night and request assistance from their parents to help them go back to sleep. There can be many reasons why a child might wake up during the night, and a sensible and informed approach on the part of parents will do much to reduce or even eliminate any stress that might arise as a result of these occurrences.

The prevalence of unusual night wakings is difficult to calculate without information on the child's daily routine and an accurate measure of his dietary and emotional stresses. One study found that twenty-five of sixty children (42 percent) had sleep disturbances, as reported by their parents.[1] The most common problem was night waking, which 22 percent of the children experienced, according to their parents. Thirteen percent of the children in this study were reported to resist bedtime, and 7 percent experienced both night waking and bedtime struggles. Although we can guess that the vast majority of these "problems" were a result of avoidable stresses, misaligned internal clocks, and lack of healthy bedtime rituals, the authors of this study noted that persistent sleep disturbances were significantly related to an increased frequency of stress factors in the environment. Additionally, 20 percent of the mothers at initial interview and 30 percent at three-year follow-up perceived their child's sleep disturbances as stressful to them and to their family life. In other words, sleep disturbances probably lead to a vicious cycle, wherein the stress that causes sleep disturbances leads to more stress, which leads to more sleep disturbances, and so forth.

On a similar note, one very troublesome study found that infants who woke up and required parental care during the night were rated as significantly more "difficult" by fathers than by mothers.[2] I think that this study reflects the problem that many fathers in our culture face: a feeling of alienation from parenthood. Both mothers and fathers may think of night wakings as a sign that their baby is "difficult" if no one has shown them how to bond effectively with their baby. Fathers in our culture have traditionally been discouraged from forming supportive, nurturing, emotionally healthy, and mutually beneficial bonds with their children. Thankfully, this is changing.

In general, though, we should remember that a child is more likely to wake up during the night and require assistance if he has been subjected to disruptive substances and influences during the day. Whatever the cause, when faced with a night-waking situation, parents need good advice on how to handle it intelligently and compassionately.

In approaching night wakings, the first thing I tell parents is that the reason why a child awakens in the night is usually related to the child's age and stage of emotional development. Consequently, the approach that parents take should reflect this fact.

Night Waking in Newborns

Prospective parents and the parents of newborn babies would be wise to prepare themselves for the biological fact that newborn babies are unable to sleep through the night. This necessarily means lost sleep for parents. It is one of the many sacrifices that parents have always made for their children. The good news is that this period of lost sleep lasts only a short time. After about two or three months, healthy babies will be sleeping for about five-hour stretches during the night. After about six months, some healthy babies will be sleeping through most nights. Wise parents know that this sacrifice is just part of being a parent. In any event, free yourself from the expectation that your baby will conform to the sleeping schedule of other babies. Instead, tenderly accept and value your baby's unique sleep pattern.

It is best to avoid fixating on your sleep loss. There is nothing you can do about it, beyond adapting your schedule to the baby's. You may be able to learn to sleep when your baby sleeps. After all, she needs to sleep a greater percentage of the day than you do. If your baby wakes when you are occupied with housework, put him in your papoose or sling and continue doing the housework together. If your baby wakes up while you are busy reading a book, pick up your baby and continue reading the book aloud or simply hold her in your arms while you read. As an adult, who is blessed with greater flexibility, you can adjust your schedule so that you can sleep when your baby sleeps.

Instead of focusing on the inconveniences presented by this period in your baby's life, focus instead on the many joys of being the parent of a newborn baby. Remember that you too were a newborn baby once. You too required about six months before you could sleep through the night. When your children are grown up and have left the house, the fondest memories you will have of them are usually those related to their babyhood. Consciously and joyously immerse yourself in the beautiful, privileged experience of being the parent of a newborn baby.

Night Waking in Older Babies

After six months, children may be excellent sleepers. If parents have helped children to foster the healthy daytime activities that correctly reset the biological clock—such as getting sufficient exposure to morning sunshine and getting adequate exercise—and if parents have been careful to protect their children from the known causes of sleep disturbances—such as caffeine, stress, and discomfort—night wakings should rarely occur. The beautiful ease with which most children sleep at night is often greatly envied by adults. For this reason, I suspect that the occasional episode of night waking is less a problem for the child than it is for the parent. The parents will typically have a much harder time getting back to sleep, whereas the child will settle back to sleep with ease.

A baby who is six months or older, for instance, who sleeps with his parent, may awaken during the night for no other reason than to reassure himself of his surroundings. He may remain perfectly quiet. Once he has felt the reassuring presence of his mother or father, the baby may fall back asleep just as silently as he awoke in the first place.

The emotional causes of the night waking may be exactly the same for babies who sleep with a parent and those who sleep alone, but the child's reactions will necessarily be different. The child's need to establish bodily contact with the parent is just as strong, but the only way for the solitary baby to signal that such contact is required is through crying.

Other older babies, for reasons that we may be unable to ascertain, may wake up and want to breast-feed. Usually this contact with the mother is less in response to a nutritional need and more in response to an emotional need. We cannot always know what is going on in a baby's mind. Additionally, unsuspected stresses encountered during the day may lead the baby to seek to reestablish emotional balance by gentle suckling at night. Mothers should support this need. Only good can come from allowing a baby to reassure herself in this positive manner.

Mistaken Approaches to Night Waking

The idea, often heard these days, that babies can and *should* learn to "self-soothe," without any physical or emotional interaction with parents, is incorrect. The best and most effective way for a child to learn to lull himself quietly back to sleep after experiencing a night waking is for parents to have demonstrated their dependability and availability when the child was a baby. Otherwise, that emotional upset the baby suffered as a result of the traumatic event that aroused him from sleep in the first place may be compounded by the terror and frustration of feeling abandoned and unwanted. If a baby learns that his mother will come to him whenever he awakens in distress and cries out for her, he is more likely to develop into a self-reliant and self-assured child who will have the ability to assess and manage his own night wakings without involving his parents unnecessarily. It cannot be overly stressed that depriving a baby or a child of emotional support when he needs or wants it runs the risk of creating an emotionally unstable child and eventually an emotionally unstable adult. Only good can come from cuddling your baby whenever he needs it. In the best of worlds, a baby would automatically receive all the cuddling he needs without ever having to ask for it.

I know how hard it is for some parents to accept this wisdom. It is directly contrary to the advice that many American parents have been given for the past few generations. It is often hard for today's parents, who may have been deprived of adequate cuddling and emotional support from their own parents when they were babies, to give that support and physical comfort to their own children. They may feel uncomfortable holding their baby or dealing with the emotional requirements of a child.

Many years ago, I had a neighbor who was a very intelligent, sensitive, and successful woman. She and her husband had just had a beautiful baby daughter, and, naturally, they wanted the very best for their baby. The baby's pediatrician was attached to the most prestigious, long-established, and well-respected HMO in her state. When that pediatrician warned the mother against ever picking up her baby when she cried lest she "spoil" her, and when he warned her never to feed the baby except at four-hour intervals, she followed that mistaken advice to the letter. This mother had the best of intentions toward her daughter. She wanted to do the right thing, but the advice she was given was so wrong as to achieve the exact opposite results. The poor baby spent almost all of her time screaming and crying alone in a playpen. This was what the doctor had ordered.

Her daughter survived all right, and she grew up to be very beautiful, but she also grew up to be an emotionally unstable, distant, and insecure young lady whose troubled relationship with her mother was a source of pain for them both. Sadly, this scenario is all too typical in our country. So many of today's adults were raised by intelligent and well-meaning parents who were given very bad advice from professionals who themselves were operating from seriously mistaken medical textbooks and medical teaching. Thankfully, this sort of antichild teaching is being challenged and scientifically debunked.

This, then, brings us to the very important issue of crying. This is a topic of great importance to many parents, and many have heard a lot of conflicting advice on this subject. I will tell you now that my approach to this issue is grounded entirely in a philosophy that recognizes the genuine emotional and physical needs of children in this situation and seeks to support them in a compassionate, loving, and scientific way.

Because of the publicity that this issue has generated, "sleep experts" have emerged to give parents two similar methods of "treatment"—both of which are unacceptable to thinking parents.

The first of these misguided "treatments" is the so-called "timed visit" or "Ferber method,"[3] otherwise known as "extinction," which attempts to use behavioral conditioning to teach children to "self-soothe." I think it is instructive to note that the frightening term *extinction* refers to the process of ignoring a baby's nighttime cries and refusing to soothe the baby. Oddly, it is the people who advocate ignoring a baby's cries who use this term.[4] The negative connotations of this word tell us that this practice is incompatible with responsible and loving parenting.

When a child wakes up and cries, advocates of extinction tell parents to enter the baby's room to check that the child is not in any "real" danger. They may reassure the baby verbally, but they are forbidden from nursing the baby or giving her any physical comfort. Then the parents are instructed to leave the child's room, even if she is still upset and crying. Against their better judgment, parents are ordered to let the baby or child "cry it out" until she goes back to sleep from exhaustion. If the child is still crying after five minutes, parents may go back and try again, but they are discouraged from touching the child. They then exit the room. If the child is still upset after ten minutes, the parents may return. If the child is still distressed and crying after fifteen minutes, they go back in briefly, but then leave the child alone for twenty minutes, and so forth. Each night after that, the amount of time before going into the child's room is increased by five minutes.

If we are to believe the self-promoting reports offered by the advocates of this method, it is usually supposed to work after a few nights. Success is measured by the reluctance of the child to call out for his parents, even if he still wakes up, needs help, or is traumatized by fear. If extinction fails to achieve the desired goals, the advocates instruct parents to wait a month and then try again.

Even if this method does stifle the cries of the child in distress, we have to ask ourselves if this is really such a good thing. The advocates of extinction have ignored the psychological impact of this sort of treatment. They measure success merely by the degree to which the child has been silenced. No one yet knows what happens in the mind of a baby who is systematically ignored and coldly bullied in this fashion. Certainly, no reasonable person can honestly believe that a baby can understand that she is being "trained" to "self-soothe" or to make a transition from a state of distress to one of relaxation. Adults know from their own experience that they themselves are unlikely to learn new tasks properly when they are crying and in a state of emotional distress.

A crying baby's needs are so simple, and they are so simply supplied. A baby cries to communicate to you his need for the touch, warmth, comfort, security, and love that only you can provide. Why would anyone deny such a simple, human request? Is a cuddle and a tender word such a hard thing that we cannot give it to a child in need? I personally believe that no normal, emotionally stable parents would put their precious baby through this sort of "conditioning" unless they were grievously misled. Sometimes I fear that some parents may be misguided into thinking that babies are just another type of pet animal, like a dog that can be trained to obey and perform simple tasks on command. It should go without saying that babies are not dogs and should not be treated as such. You cannot "train" a baby to obey your orders. A baby comes into this world "knowing" exactly what his needs are. Meeting these needs in an intelligent, humane, and loving manner is the only way to ensure that your child progresses smoothly through the biologically determined stages of human development.

The other popular method that some "sleep experts" advocate is the "sleeping partner" method. If the baby awakens in the night and cries out for her parents, one of the parents is instructed to go to the child's room and lie down somewhere in the room, but not in the same bed. An improvement in "sleep behavior" is supposed to happen after three or four nights. The baby is supposed to accept the "sentence" of sleep without protest. Somehow the baby is supposed to understand that the parents expect her to sleep through the night. Somehow the baby is supposed to understand that, if she wakes up because she happens to be thirsty, because she just needs to be reminded that her parents are still there and that they love her, or because she is frightened by a nightmare, she is to keep still and refrain from bothering anyone.

I have heard at lectures and read in books by "sleep experts" that these methods work 80 to 90 percent of the time, but my own clinical experience with parents who come to my office in Los Angeles demonstrates to me that these methods are largely ineffective and certainly do not work at a rate as high as the "experts" claim.

Regarding a child as if he were nothing more than an animal to be trained is a grave mistake. We really have little idea what kind of long-term damage we are doing to our babies when we treat them this way. When a baby fails to call out for his parents when he is in distress at night, it cannot be because he has "learned" a useful behavior. It is more likely that he has just given up on his parents. Psychological defense mechanisms erect a wall between the child and his parents. I can think of few things sadder than a child who can no longer love his parents but fears and distrusts them instead. In all of nature, there is no mammalian species in which the mother fails to respond immediately to her infant's cries. Despite their superior intelligence, only humans can be tricked into endangering the health, happiness, and welfare of their own offspring.

It is helpful for parents to remind themselves that babies and young children are emotional rather than rational creatures. A child cannot comprehend why you are ignoring his cries for help. Ignoring your baby's cries, even with the best of intentions, may lead him to feel that he has been abandoned. The result will be an insecure and unhappy child. You cannot "spoil" a child by responding to his cries. Children are "spoiled" by being ignored. If they cannot get your attention through the usual means, they will resort to unpleasant behavior to get it. The more you ignore your children, the more unpleasant their behavior will become, and the more "spoiled" they will appear. The lesson you are teaching is that you value bad behavior more than good behavior. I am sure that all parents will realize the undesirability of any child learning such a lesson.

Expecting a crying baby or a young child who has experienced a night waking to "self-soothe" without any positive and nurturing interaction from you is unreasonable and ineffective. Responding to a child's cries, comforting her, and lovingly trying to help her overcome whatever is bothering her is not only effective, it is the only proper way to soothe and calm a child in order to help her fall back asleep. A crying baby wants the calming presence of a parent precisely because the baby instinctively knows that the presence of a comforting parent is the solution to her problem. Unless the parent makes himself available to the baby, the baby will not be calmed. Babies are responding to biological needs that sleep "experts" either ignore or deny.

It is true that a baby whose crying is ignored may eventually fall back asleep, but the problem that caused the night waking in the first place has remained unsolved. Even if parents have checked to make sure that the baby is not sick or in physical discomfort, unless they pick up the baby, interact with him in a compassionate way, soothe him, or nurse him until he falls back asleep, the underlying or accompanying emotional stress will remain. The emotional stresses of a baby do not simply go away if they are ignored. They multiply and may lead to long-term disorders in the relationship between parent and child. Meeting your baby's emotional needs by answering his cries and interacting with him, therefore, is the approach of choice for parents.

Remember that babies cry for a reason. We may not always know what the reason is, and we may not always be able to solve the problem, but we can always try. If a baby cries at night, it may be because she is hungry, thirsty, sick, cold, hot, uncomfortable, agitated, lonely, or frightened by a nightmare. Whatever the problem is, the fact that the baby cries indicates that the baby is unable to solve the problem alone. She requires the assistance of her parents. Let us also remember that babies cry only as a last resort, after all other means of trying to establish communication with the parents have failed. A child's crying in response to a night waking, therefore, can represent an intensification of the initial stress that caused the waking in the first place. Consequently, the most sensible and compassionate approach is to respond immediately to your child's cries. Babies do not cry because they have nothing better to do or because they are trying to annoy you. They cry because they are in real distress. When your baby cries, she is calling *you*. She is requesting your assistance the only way she knows how. After all, a child who has awakened at night and begins to cry may be sick, in discomfort, in danger, or in pain. You will not be able to assess the situation until you go to your baby and hold her in your arms.

Sensible and Effective Approaches to Common Night Waking and Other Sleep Problems

If your child awakens in the night and needs you, go to him. If your child shares a bed with you, hold him in your arms and be there for him. Remind yourself that you are the parent, and that giving your baby reassurance is one of the joyous responsibilities of being a parent. It is a beautiful feeling knowing that you alone have the power to brighten your child's life and banish fear and sorrow. In your child's eyes, you are a miraculous, godlike being. Show your child that you are worthy of the high esteem in which he holds you.

The object in handling night wakings is to reestablish as quickly as possible the necessary conditions for restful and secure sleep. Avoid turning on any lights or doing anything that will excite your child. Speak softly and gently. Once you have ministered to the physical or emotional needs that precipitated the waking, hug, cuddle, or stroke your precious child until she falls back asleep. If your child needs the additional security of coming into your bed, let her come in with you. There are a variety of valid reasons why children may want to sleep with you on occasion. If co-sleeping is not the usual arrangement in your family and if circumstances make it difficult for you to consider soothing your child in this simple and natural way, cuddle your child or quietly rub her back until she falls back asleep in her own bed. The greater your willingness to invest a little time in your child at these moments, the greater the chances that she will fall back asleep quickly and stay asleep.

Nightmares

One common cause of night wakings is nightmares. A child who experiences a nightmare that is disturbing and frightening enough actually to wake the child from a deep sleep and leave him in a state of distress is a child who will benefit from a parent's comfort.

The younger the child is, the less he will be able to distinguish dreams from reality in general. This is because children are emotional rather than intellectual creatures. The emotions that humans of all ages feel in dreams are real emotions generated by the emotional centers of the brain. Consequently, the aftereffects of these emotions are real, physical events, even if the experiences that provoked the emotional response happened in the dream state. We adults can apply reason to mitigate the emotional effects of nightmares, but children generally cannot do so.

When your child wakes up in the middle of the night from a nightmare and calls out for you, go to him and soothe him. You would be wise to avoid insisting that the nightmare was "just a dream," because, to the child, it was a real experience. Children, especially younger children, will argue with you vigorously on this point. You simply cannot win this argument. Just hold your child in your arms, rock him back and forth, and reassure him that everything is all right, that you are there for him, and that he is safe. It is probably a good idea to avoid asking young children to relate the nightmare to you. This will have the undesired effect of reinforcing the experience and making it harder for your child to get back to sleep. It also runs the risk of the child's mind making a subconscious association between sleep and the negative emotions suffered during the nightmare. If your child volunteers to relate the content of the nightmare, listen sympathetically and uncritically and offer all the reassurances I mentioned above.

Older children whose intellectual faculties are more developed generally do not believe that the event experienced in the nightmare was a real event, but they too benefit from the comfort that a parent can provide at this time of distress. Fostering an emotionally stable, mentally healthy, responsible, self-reliant, and self-sufficient child requires, in part, that parents provide the necessary emotional support.

There can be a variety of causes of nightmares. One primary cause is the mental exhaustion brought on by periodic or chronic sleep debt. Make sure your child gets to bed early enough every night—especially on school nights—so that she gets the full amount of sleep that permits her to feel refreshed upon awakening in the morning and to remain alert and cheerful all day long without any sign of drowsiness. Emotional disturbances, stress, and conflicts can also induce nightmares. These conditions are only aggravated by sleep debt. Whatever the cause, whenever they occur, give your child the emotional support she needs. Cuddle and reassure your child with the same loving kindness that you would want if you were in her place.

Night Terrors

In a night terror, the child suddenly sits up during sleep with his eyes open and screams in terror. The child seems to be awake, but he is actually still asleep and is unaware of his surroundings. He eventually returns to a calm sleep. Typically, night terrors occur during deep sleep (Stages III and IV throughout the episode). Although night terrors can be disturbing to those who witness them, they are almost always forgotten by the child. Most children with night terrors outgrow them by puberty, which suggests that they are related to a delayed maturation of the central nervous system.

Like sleepwalking, there appears to be a genetic propensity toward night terrors.[5]

Night terrors occur in adults as well, and they are similar to the night terrors that occur in children, but they frequently occur in adults with histories of psychopathology.[6] Psychiatrists tell us that while adult sleepwalkers show a high incidence of personality disorders with generally active, outward behavioral patterns, adult night terror sufferers are mostly anxious, depressed, and phobic, with an inhibition of outward expression of aggression.[7]

Although drugs have been used in the past to treat night terrors,[8] no treatment is necessary for children. If, however, the night terrors occur with such frequency, pitch, and duration that some sort of intervention seems necessary, hypnosis has been very successful in preventing recurrences.[9,10] The best advice I can give parents is to relax and avoid worrying if your child experiences sleep terrors. They shall pass.

Bed-Wetting

About 85 percent of children will achieve nighttime continence about six months after they have achieved daytime continence. This usually occurs at about age three or four. For the remaining 15 percent who continue to wet the bed past age five, there is generally nothing to worry about. Studies have shown that the tendency toward bed-wetting is genetic: It runs in families.[11,12] If your child is still wetting the bed after the age of five, be very sure to provide lots of emotional support. Children do not wet the bed deliberately: Their brains simply have not yet developed the ability to respond appropriately to the signals that the full bladder is sending. Bed-wetting is not an emotional or a behavioral "problem." It is usually just a matter of an immature nervous system.

It is sad to think that in the past so many children were actually punished by misguided parents for wetting the bed. It is also a very sad reflection on the history of medicine in this country that throughout most of the twentieth century, circumcision—actually cutting off part of the penis—was touted as a preventive, cure, and *punishment* for bed-wetting. Thankfully, we are moving away from such unenlightened practices.

Sometimes, rare occurrences of bed-wetting are the result of emotional stresses that your child has experienced during the day. Additionally, children who are born with either internal or external genital malformations may experience incontinence as a result of these malformations. Whatever the cause, reassure your child that you understand it is not his fault that he has wet the bed. Remind him gently that he is not to worry and that he will soon outgrow this phase.

Bed-wetting, of course, can be very unpleasant for children, and the discomfort that it causes usually leads to night wakings. Handle this by getting up and helping your child to change out of her wet pajamas. Gently wash off any residual urine from her skin with a damp cloth. Cheerfully remove the wet bed sheets and replace them with fresh ones. Older children can probably learn to accomplish these tasks by themselves without disturbing you. Younger children, however, may be traumatized by being awakened in the first place. If this is the case, they may benefit from a little additional soothing and compassion.

Rare occurrences of bed-wetting are probably unimportant, but frequent or regular occurrences that are unrelated to medical or emotional conditions are best dealt with by taking sensible precautions. Have your child's mattress fitted with a plastic liner that lies between the mattress and the sheets. It is also a good idea to place a good, absorbent pad on top of the plastic liner and under the bottom sheet.

Prevention of bed-wetting is also important. Even children who have enjoyed years of nocturnal continence may experience an episode of bed-wetting if they have been subjected to undue stresses during the day. So many of these stresses, however, are dietary. Help your child to avoid eating dinner or drinking beverages too close to bedtime. Caffeinated drinks should be especially avoided at nighttime, as these dramatically increase the need to urinate.

It is also a good idea to encourage your child to go to the lavatory one last time before slipping into bed. I suspect that so much of the reluctance all of us occasionally feel at the prospect of one last trip to the lavatory is due, in part, to the physical discomfort of most lavatories. The cold tile floors and the cold toilet seat are as uninviting to sleepy children as to adults. You can easily mitigate these conditions by placing a small, clean area rug in front of the toilet to protect bare feet from cold tiles. Old-fashioned wooden toilet seats are also much warmer than the usual plastic or laminated seats. These are among the simple, small, and inexpensive changes you can make to your home environment that will help both you and your child get an undisturbed, peaceful night's sleep.

Sleep Apnea

Sleep apnea is a fairly rare condition that almost never affects normal, healthy babies or children. *Sleep apnea* refers to a condition in which breathing stops, usually as a result of obstruction of the air passages, and almost always is accompanied by adverse changes in the nervous system, heart, and blood circulation. Babies suffering from a severe episode of apnea will turn bluish. Apnea of this severity is a medical emergency requiring immediate attention. Most episodes of apnea, however, seem to do little harm and will disappear as the baby develops.

The contributing factors to apnea may be weak chest muscles or, more commonly, a buildup of mucus that the baby is unable to cough out. Once the underlying condition that causes the apnea is cleared up, sleep apnea usually disappears.

True obstructive sleep apnea may stem from enlarged adenoids and tonsils, but it is usually related to craniofacial anomalies. Other risk factors include obesity and neuromuscular disease.[13] During sleep, infants with obstructive sleep apneas may snore, experience laborious breathing, and sweat profusely.[14] While they are awake, they may have breath-holding spells. During feeding, they may have difficulty swallowing.[15] Abnormal weight, difficult growth, and recurring ear infections may also develop. The obstructed breaths occur mainly in REM and light, non-REM sleep. Premature babies are more likely to suffer from apnea than healthy older infants. Among older children and adolescents, obesity seems to be a major cause of sleep apnea.[16]

Sleep apnea should be distinguished from a similar but harmless phenomenon called *periodic breathing*. Sleeping infants may cease breathing for periods up to ten seconds. This causes no harm and is just a stage of lung development. Babies soon outgrow periodic breathing.

Apnea is more commonly seen in obese adults who snore. The reason they do not usually die is that the brain wakes them up during the episode so that they are startled back into regular breathing. Unfortunately, the moment they fall back asleep, the cycle of apnea resumes. Adults who suffer from apnea almost never remember the multiple wakings during the night, but because they have been unable to reach deep sleep, they will be exhausted during the day.

The great danger of apnea, however, is its very close association with *sudden infant death syndrome* (SIDS). It is very likely that the dangerous practice of putting babies to sleep on their abdomen contributes to obstruction of the air passages, which, in turn, can lead to SIDS.

Another important contributing factor to sleep apnea in infants is exposure to secondhand tobacco smoke.[17] Pregnant women who smoke or who are exposed to secondhand tobacco smoke are also more likely to give birth to underweight babies who are prone to apnea.[18,19] Environmental tobacco smoke exposure also represents a significant contributing factor to another sleep problem, *gastroesophageal reflux* (GER).[20] GER is a fancy medical term for the common phenomenon of spitting up, which almost all babies do from time to time, but it can be a potentially life-threatening situation if it occurs while a baby is asleep. It not only causes pain, but it can cause babies to choke.

Certainly, you already know that there are many good reasons to protect unborn babies and children from exposure to tobacco smoke. It is imperative that any and all smokers in your household cease this habit when you find out you are pregnant or, better still, the moment you decide to have children. We all agree that smokers have a right to smoke, but we must also agree that smokers have no right to impose their smoke on others, especially those who are too young to defend themselves. If all the smoke from a cigarette went into a smoker's lungs and stayed there, no one could raise any objections. Unfortunately, smokers create a cloud of noxious fumes that imperil the health and hygiene of anyone who comes near them. Unborn babies, newborns, and children of all ages deserve to be raised in a smoke-free environment.

Sleep apnea may be caused by "enlarged" tonsils or adenoids, and obviously, cutting out these organs can cure sleep apnea and prevent snoring. Still, this is not a rational solution. The myth that the enlargement of the tonsils and adenoids in children is a pathological condition was spread through a misunderstanding on the part of the medical profession in the late nineteenth century and the first three-quarters of the twentieth century. Science has now recognized that all children have tonsils and adenoids that are proportionally larger than those of adults. The tonsils reach their maximum size between the ages of five and six. This is very convenient, because this is precisely the age at which your child will usually come into contact with large numbers of other children at nursery schools, play groups, or kindergarten. This immersion into the wider society of children of the same age is also an immersion into a large sea of previously unencountered germs.

Both the tonsils and the adenoids are an important part of the immune system, playing a major role in protecting us from disease and infection. Indeed, they are on the front line of defense against viral pathogens. Even if the tonsils are genuinely inflamed, this is probably an indication that your child is being bombarded with an extra-heavy load of pathogenic viruses. Your child's immune system is working overtime to build up immunity to all the new strains of virus that it is encountering. Every effort should be made to conserve and preserve tonsils in this situation. Wartime is hardly the time to throw away your weapons.

Whole generations of American children may well have survived the mass routine tonsillectomies of the past, but science has barely begun to document the long-term effects caused by the loss of such a central part of the immune system. Sometimes we forget that modern medicine is blessed with a wide array of antibiotics, which, when properly used, can obviate the need for surgical amputations. It just does not make sense to amputate an infected body part when antibiotics can so easily clear up the infection. It certainly does not make sense to amputate a part of the immune system. Even in those extremely rare instances where the tonsils actually are causing obstruction of the air passages, it is best to wait. After the age of six, the tonsils should decrease in size automatically and allow greater freedom of breathing.

Snoring

We usually associate snoring with middle-age men, but it can occur in infants and children too. Parents may be very concerned when they notice that their baby snores, and, indeed, their concern is sometimes well founded because snoring in infants and children is a common sign of upper airway obstruction.[21] In most children, however, primary snoring rarely leads to obstructive sleep apnea syndrome.[22]

There are many causes of snoring in children. Enlarged adenoids or tonsils may cause snoring in some cases,[23] but this is usually a temporary phenomenon without medical importance. Often, children who snore also have allergies. Furthermore, allergies are associated with an increased risk of obstructive sleep apnea syndrome.[24]

The prevalence of snoring varies widely and seems to be related to environmental factors. For instance, 27 percent of children in the town of Frome, Somerset, in England habitually snore,[25] but only 16.7 percent of children in the town of Gardabaer in Iceland habitually snore.[26] In Frome, the rate of snoring increased to 47 percent when the children had an upper respiratory infection. This study also found that snoring was significantly associated with a history of poor hearing, restless sleep, having a cold, parental smoking, eczema, sleeptalking, moving around the bed at night, sore throats, having a runny nose, and mouth breathing. The message here is that if you live in a cold, windy, and foggy part of the world where respiratory infections are common, your child may be more likely to snore than a child who lives in a temperate, dry, sunny, and healthy climate.

If your child snores when he has a cold, there is little to worry about, but if the snoring persists even when he is healthy, you might want to bring this to the attention of your child's pediatrician. If the cause really seems to be enlarged adenoids or tonsils, the best approach is to just wait and see. As I have mentioned, these organs will eventually reduce in size by themselves. It is better to wait and put up with a little snoring than to remove these organs and force the child to go through the rest of his life without the benefits that these organs confer.

Sleepwalking

Sleepwalking is not really a medical condition, but it can alarm some parents. I should point out that sleepwalking is not really a type of night waking because the sleepwalker is actually still asleep, though not dreaming.

Sleepwalking is not as uncommon as you might think. Fifteen out of 100 children between the ages of six and sixteen experience episodes of sleepwalking from time to time.[27] Often it can be related to heightened levels of stress, but usually sleepwalking is unrelated to emotional troubles. Additionally, there is strong evidence that the propensity to sleepwalk is inherited.[28]

Sleepwalkers usually wander about, aware of their surroundings, though still technically asleep, for about thirty minutes before returning to bed. Should you come across a sleepwalking child, gently guide her back to her bed. It is best to avoid trying to awaken her, as she will be very disoriented and may become frightened. Sleepwalkers almost never remember having walked in their sleep. The phenomenon usually disappears by age fifteen. Medical or psychological treatment is unnecessary.[29]

The best thing that you can do for your sleepwalking child is to make your house as secure as possible. Keep your floors clear of any objects over which a sleepwalker might trip and fall. Install safety gates at the top of stairways, and make sure that windows are securely shut and draped. The precautions you take will depend on the features of your house. Use your own good sense to prevent accidents.

Sleeptalking

Sleeptalking, like sleepwalking, occurs during the nondreaming stages of deep sleep, most often in the transition between non-REM sleep to REM sleep. Sleeptalking has no importance, and the words uttered rarely form coherent sentences. Sleeptalkers never remember having talked in their sleep. This is because the talking does not take place within the context of a dream that might be remembered.

Night-Eating Syndrome

A phenomenon related to sleepwalking is the very rare night-eating syndrome. The sleepwalker will walk to a source of food—usually a refrigerator—and begin eating until he is full. He then returns to bed. Upon waking in the morning, he is entirely unaware of having enjoyed a nighttime feast. Night eating can often be a contributing cause of obesity,[30] although, obviously, not all obese children experience night-eating syndrome. Binge eating during the day and night eating are overlapping but different behaviors. Night-eating syndrome appears to be fully independent of an unhealthy preoccupation with food and dieting.[31]

Treatment of night-eating syndrome is problematic. It is so rare in children that I have been unable to find any published studies offering any suggestions. Cognitive-behavioral therapies have been found to be ineffective for obese adults who suffer from the syndrome, but pharmacotherapy has been very effective in controlling night eating and inducing loss of excess weight. These medications often consist of a dopaminergic agent taken with codeine at bedtime.[32] If your child is obese or is suffering from other eating disorders, you will, undoubtedly, already have her under a doctor's care. Be sure to bring the night-eating syndrome to your doctor's attention.

If your child is otherwise healthy and still engages in night eating while sleepwalking, it would be best to avoid resorting to drugs. Use your ingenuity to discover ways of blocking access to the source of food. Putting a lock on the food pantry or blocking the door to the refrigerator may help.

Tooth Grinding

Tooth grinding during sleep can be very worrying to observers. It is loud and grating. Thankfully, it is harmless, though you might mention it to your child's dentist just to reassure yourself that no damage has been done. Many parents assume that tooth grinding must be related to emotional troubles and stress, but it is, in fact, a harmless, transitory phenomenon.

Children who grind their teeth during sleep, like sleeptalkers and sleep-walkers, have no idea they are doing it. Also, like sleeptalking, tooth grinding occurs during the transition between non-REM to REM sleep. Most children who grind their teeth during sleep outgrow it before they reach adulthood.

Strange Movements During Sleep

Some children may experience other odd movements during the transition from non-REM to REM sleep. I know of one boy who routinely and gracefully pops his knuckles in his sleep. Other children may kick their legs or move their arms in unusual ways. These movements are not of any importance, even though anyone who sleeps with the child may find them disquieting.

Rocking

Some babies may engage in odd episodes of rhythmic, repetitive rocking or head banging during sleep. Babies seem to do this as a way of calming themselves to sleep. I suspect that this sort of behavior is a message to us of the great value of carrying your baby in a sling or papoose. The rocking motion that the baby experiences while being carried lulls her to sleep. It seems that the evolutionary adaptation that enables babies to fall asleep while in motion also sometimes requires that babies *be* in motion to fall asleep. Sometimes, I think we have forgotten the wisdom of our ancestors, who not only carried their babies on their backs but also rocked children to sleep in rocking cradles or in their arms while sitting in a rocking chair. Science, in fact, has documented that rhythmic rocking is protective against SIDS.[33]

Whatever the case, rhythmic, repetitive rocking or head banging is not a real medical condition and is not necessarily a symptom of autism or other neurological disorders. Indeed, the reason that autistic children rock back and forth is precisely because it has a calming effect.

Most children who rock back and forth during sleep outgrow it by age two. Since there is nothing you can do to prevent it, you can at least make it as harmless as possible by making sure that your baby's sleeping area is as safe as possible and free of sharp objects or sharp edges or corners that could cause bodily harm. Even if your baby does not practice rhythmic rocking or head-banging movements, you should take these precautions as a matter of course.

Restless Leg Syndrome

Restless leg syndrome (RLS) is extremely rare in children, being more commonly found in the elderly or those suffering from a debilitating brain disease such as Parkinson's disease. RLS is characterized by unusual sensations in the muscles and bones of the lower legs. These sensations are difficult for the sufferer to describe. They occur most frequently in bed at night, and normally disappear when the patient gets up and starts moving. The cause is unknown, and the incidence is thought to be 5 percent.[34] RLS is the fourth most frequent cause of insomnia in elderly adults.

In the extremely unlikely event that your child is genuinely suffering from restless leg syndrome, seek the advice of your pediatrician, who may refer you to a specialist. Unfortunately, the treatments available for young patients all involve powerful drugs that alter brain chemistry, such as the benzodiazepines (especially clonazepam).[35]

Insomnia

Most of us, on at least one occasion, have had the unpleasant experience of passing what appears to be a sleepless night in bed. Usually, the cause is stress or worry. Other causes are medications, drugs, caffeine, pain, or illness. Often, the perception of having never fallen asleep is incorrect. We may actually have slept most of the night, experiencing several periods of remembered wakefulness, but our stress and worries have so dominated our thoughts and dreams that the periods of sleep are unremembered. Most self-diagnosed insomniacs actually sleep quite well. It is only their self-awareness that is disordered. Someone who has truly been denied the requisite amount of sleep will be extremely drowsy during the day and will nod off at the earliest opportunity. Most self-professed insomniacs are fully alert during the day, thus proving that they really do sleep even if they do not think they do.

If true insomnia is rare among adults, it is even rarer among children. True insomnia, indeed, is not a disease itself, but a symptom of some other problem. There are, of course, those occasions when children are unable to fall asleep or they awaken in the middle of the night, unable to fall back asleep, but, as in adults, these episodes are almost always related to caffeine consumption, stress, worry, conflict, or discomforts of many kinds. A noisy house, strange surroundings, an uncomfortable mattress, sickness, pain, poor diet, and bad digestion are just some of the factors that can cause a child to lose sleep. The successful treatment of sleeplessness in children, then, is the elimination of the causes.

Some children are unable to sleep at night because their internal clock is misaligned. They may be napping during the day, thereby paying off their sleep debt at an inopportune time. Discouraging naps and setting and maintaining a regular morning rising time and evening bedtime are simple ways of resetting the internal clock so that children will sleep during the night.

In the hotter climates around the Mediterranean, the afternoon siesta would seem at first glance to be a potent source of misalignment of the internal clock, but it is a necessity dictated by culture and climate. Because the extreme heat of the afternoon sun makes it difficult to spend the afternoon productively, Mediterranean cultures evolved a strategy of sleeping during the afternoon, which enables them to be productive in the evening. In Sicily, for instance, the evening meal may not be taken until 9:00 or even 10:00. In these climates, it is still too hot at 6:00 to consider firing up the oven or standing over a hot stove preparing dinner. The only way that children or adults can get the sleep they need is to break up the daily sleep cycle into a long period after midnight and a shorter period during the afternoon. In the temperate climes, such as most of the United States and northern Europe, it is not necessary to divide sleep like this; thus, afternoon naps are neither necessary nor advised for children who will be going to bed at 9:00 and will be expected to stay alert throughout the day.

Some children, however, genuinely suffer from clinical insomnia, but these children are usually suffering from some neurological disorder for which insomnia is either a symptom or a side effect of the pharmacological treatment. These disorders include attention-deficit hyperactivity disorder (ADHD),[36] obsessive-compulsive disorder,[37] depressive disorders,[38] epilepsy,[39] and autism.[40] Insomnia may also result as a side effect from the drugs sometimes used to manage asthma.[41] If your child is afflicted with one of these problems, he will undoubtedly already be under a doctor's care. Do bring the insomnia to the doctor's attention, but be aware that it may be difficult to solve.

I am sorry to report that some doctors prescribe drugs to treat perfectly healthy and normal children who seem to be suffering from "insomnia." One study found that children (especially boys) for whom drugs have been prescribed for "insomnia" are very likely to have parents (especially mothers) who themselves take sleeping pills because of "insomnia."[42] These parents seem to be projecting their own perceived illnesses on to their children. It is important that doctors identify these unfortunate familial patterns of drug consumption, discourage them, and encourage drug-free approaches to nocturnal sleeplessness, should it really exist.

Similarly, it has long been observed that parents tend to overestimate and overreport the frequency of their children's sleep problems, regardless of whether such problems really exist. Sleep laboratory studies have shown that children identified by their parents as "good sleepers" actually wake up just as frequently during the night as children who were identified by their parents as "poor sleepers."[43] The difference is that the good sleepers managed to fall back asleep without involving their parents.

The message, then, is that parents would do themselves and their children a favor by adopting a positive and optimistic attitude toward their children's sleep and by fostering good sleep habits in their children from birth by demonstrating their availability, dependability, reliability, and reasonability. Parents can do no better than to reassure themselves and their children that sleep disturbances occasionally occur and that most minor sleep problems are unimportant. Most sleep problems are easily prevented by taking sensible precautions. Be of good cheer, remind yourself of the value of being flexible, and, above all, show your children how much you love them.

Chapter 3

Common Things That Impair a Healthy Night's Sleep and How You Can Avoid Them

*A*long with all the things that you can do to help your child get a good night's sleep, there are plenty of things that you and your child should avoid to help foster healthy sleep patterns. Many are just a matter of good sense, but others may make you pause for thought.

As I have pointed out elsewhere in this book, for most children who suffer from nonpathological sleep disturbances, the problem is not with sleeping through the night but with falling asleep in the first place. It is important to avoid those elements that disrupt normal bodily cycles and rhythms. It is equally important to avoid those factors that alter the brain's chemistry or induce a state of agitation or emotional imbalance. Today, it is sometimes difficult for parents to take a stand against many of these things, but take a stand they must.

Avoiding the things that upset your child's internal clock and make falling asleep and staying asleep difficult is just as important as promoting the simple things—such as exposure to morning sun and exercise—that correctly reset the internal clock. I believe that the vast majority of caring parents who use their native good sense will naturally help their children avoid whatever disturbs sleep.

As an example, consider Allan, a bright twelve-year-old boy, who was recently on a summer holiday in Europe. Allan made his holiday especially enjoyable by sampling the local chocolate wherever he went. His parents knew that the caffeine in chocolate was a concern, but they did not want to deny Allan the pleasure of this "culinary" experience. Allan enjoyed comparing the differences in sweetness, richness, bitterness, and smoothness among the chocolate bars he found in various countries. Unfortunately, he developed severe migraine headaches in the evenings, headaches so severe that they prevented him from sleeping. Allan had always suffered from migraines, but no one had suspected that chocolate could have been the source of the trouble. After one of his evening migraines, he would arise the next morning unrested, exhausted, and irritable. At the suggestion of a friend who was traveling with him, Allan went without chocolate for a day. At the end of the day, he was free of all headaches. He so enjoyed the freedom from this debilitating pain that he voluntarily went without chocolate for several more days. The headaches were gone, and he enjoyed the best sleep he could ever remember having. A few days later, as an experiment, he ate a chocolate bar in the afternoon. Sure enough, that evening Allan was suffering from a major migraine. He was unable to sleep because of the pain. He was now convinced that there was a direct link between his consumption of chocolate and his migraines. None of his brothers or sisters had the same reaction to chocolate, but that, of course, was unimportant. Allan and his parents realized that it was better for his sleep and his health in general if he trusted his good sense and acknowledged that chocolate, in his case, brought on headaches.

This is an example of an intelligent child and his caring parents using their good sense and making the right decision. Still, even the most intelligent and caring parents can be inadvertently misled into making poor decisions, such as giving children over-the-counter drugs. The influence of advertising cannot be overestimated in our market-driven society. Furthermore, many good and loving parents have, I am sorry to say, received poor advice from uninformed doctors. Thankfully, the growing field of sleep science has already produced a large body of scientific literature with which pediatricians are supposed to be familiar. Increasingly, the mistaken medical advice that was common in past generations is gradually being forgotten. As more and more doctors learn that sleeping pills, for instance, are inappropriate for children and that other common things—such as caffeine—have a detrimental effect on children's sleep, this information will be passed on to parents. The beneficiaries will be children as well as parents, for both will be able to develop and maintain healthy sleep habits.

Avoiding Drugs

Drugs such as phenobarbital, Valium, or other sleep-inducing medications should never be given to children of any age. In the past, doctors routinely used to make the mistake of prescribing such medications to babies and children. Nowadays, doctors should know better, but a parent must remain vigilant. If a doctor prescribes such medications, get a second opinion. Obviously, if your child is suffering from a neurological disorder, such as epilepsy or obsessive-compulsive disorder, whose treatment requires the prescription of mind-altering, insomnia-causing drugs that must be used in conjunction with sleeping pills, you may not have any choice, but for otherwise healthy children, drugs should be avoided. These brain-altering chemicals are dangerous on their own and can quickly become addictive. If your child's sleeping difficulties are so severe that you are tempted to medicate your child with your own prescription or over-the-counter sleeping pills, call a doctor and/or a family counselor. Drugs are not an option for common sleep problems.

Because sleeping pills are so common, people make the mistake of thinking they are harmless and that they are useful for children. Every night, more than 13 million adult Americans resort to prescribed medicine to assist them in falling asleep, and many more medicate themselves with over-the-counter remedies. These drugs, which are sometimes very potent, can cause "rebound insomnia," disrupt REM sleep, or have other significant side effects. They may cause a distressing dependence on chemicals in order to fall asleep and stay asleep. We do not want our children to suffer from such addictions.

The most commonly used sedative/hypnotic medications are in a class of drugs called benzodiazepines, of which the most widely used are diazepam (Valium), lorazepam (Ativan), temazepam (Restoril), estazolam (ProSom), and triazolam (Halcion). It would be good to familiarize yourself with these names so that you can be alert if anyone tries to prescribe such drugs for your child. These drugs all act on the central nervous system to produce sedation, hypnosis, muscle relaxation, and decreased anxiety. Although they are rarely indicated on genuine medical grounds, these drugs are commonly prescribed for the treatment of insomnia in adults. If prescribed for adults, they should not be used more than three to four times a week. They are not indicated for solving children's sleep problems.

Zolpidem (Ambien) has become the latest popular drug for inducing sleep in adults, but it too should not be given to children. Zolpidem is probably too new for any untoward reactions to have been evaluated. Barbiturates such as phenobarbital were once the most commonly used drugs to induce sleep but are no longer indicated for adults or children, as they are very easily abused, are addicting, and have many other unpleasant effects.

Neither babies nor children should be given the familiar "pink liquid"—elixir of phenobarbital—to quiet them down. Neither should parents give their children the other familiar pink liquid—Benadryl elixir—to induce sleep. This antihistamine is sold without a prescription and is an ingredient of many over-the-counter products sold to adults to help them sleep.

The idea of putting a child to sleep with a "sleeping potion" is a very old and a very bad idea. Many older medical textbooks recommended sleep remedies, such as paregoric, tincture of laudanum, and other drugs derived from the opium poppy. Of course, I hope that we would never do anything as absurd as this in the twenty-first century. Today, we are rightly saying no to drugs. We should stop thinking that we can solve our children's sleep problems with chemicals. Drugs, whether legal or illegal, foreign or domestic, herbal or natural, homeopathic or naturopathic, purchased at the pharmacy or the health food store, are not the answer to a good night's sleep for children.

Even for adults, dependence on sleeping pills can be a vicious cycle. For the sake of their children, parents who depend on sleeping pills would be wise to break that dependency. Thankfully, there is hope. An interesting study published in the medical journal *Archives of Internal Medicine*[1] found that by reestablishing the body's natural daily rhythm of melatonin—a powerful regulatory "sleep hormone" produced in the pineal gland of the brain—practitioners can help patients free themselves from long-term dependence on benzodiazepines—the potentially addictive prescription drugs commonly used to treat insomnia. The study found that long-term use of benzodiazepines may impair the endogenous melatonin rhythm, which may in turn induce or aggravate sleep disturbances. One of the major side effects of these drugs is that they suppress dreams. This can cause negative effects such as feelings of chronic bereavement, depression, and stress disorders. These, in turn, can cause or worsen insomnia. No adult and certainly no child should be subjected to such side effects, especially when sensible alternatives to sleeping problems exist.

The discovery of the important role of the brain hormone melatonin in sleep cycles is important for our purposes, because it is known that melatonin production is stimulated and regulated by sunlight. It is so simple to avoid sleep disturbances in the first place by making sure your child gets adequate exposure to sunlight every day, engages in the other simple activities that promote good sleep, and avoids those common things that disrupt sleep.

Avoiding Alcohol

It may seem unnecessary to suggest that parents should refrain from giving their children alcohol, but sadly, in our diverse society, some misinformed parents mistakenly give their infants and children small amounts of bourbon, scotch, gin, wine, or beer, thinking that this is an acceptable way to induce sleep. Others apply small amounts of alcohol to the gums while babies are teething. Alcohol in any form and in any amount is inappropriate for infants and children. It easily sets up an abusive dependency and, furthermore, is illegal to serve to children. Always read the label on anything you give a child. Many over-the-counter medications from the pharmacy, as well as homeopathic remedies and natural herbal preparations from the health food store, contain alcohol, sometimes in very large amounts.

Leaving aside the legality of alcohol for a moment, it is a scientific fact that, even though alcohol may help some people relax, it cannot help anyone—especially a child—sleep. The consumption of alcohol results in restless, agitated, fragmented sleep. These unpleasant effects, so frequently seen in adults who drink alcohol, are magnified in children. Please do not give your children alcohol. If your child's sleep disorders are so severe as to tempt you to give your child alcohol, see a doctor immediately.

Avoiding Television

In our society, it may seem futile for me to advocate that parents limit the amount of television their children watch and avoid all television before bedtime, but it is important that they do this. Television has a powerful influence over all of our lives, but its impact on children is greater than we can imagine. Television is not necessarily a bad thing, and, in fact, it can be a wonderful, informative tool that can enrich our lives, but so often it is misused and allowed to become a dangerous nuisance. In so many instances, busy, misinformed, frustrated, or uninspired parents use the television as a surrogate parent. Children can easily sit quietly in front of a television for hours if given the opportunity, but this does not mean they should or that this is harmless.

It is a sad comment on our society that, on average, American children today spend as many hours each week watching television as they do in school.[2] Study after study has shown that children's television-viewing habits are associated with a large range of problems, including obesity and poor eating habits,[3] decreased physical activity and physical fitness,[4] and poor school performance.[5] Also, the scientific literature has repeatedly documented the worrying association between children's exposure to violent images on television and later violent behavior.[6,7] One large-scale study on the effect of television on the family found, not surprisingly, that immoderate television viewing decreases the amount of time that a family might otherwise enjoyably and profitably spend interacting socially.[8] It replaces conversation with mute and mindless staring. These are just a few of the things that should concern parents about television.

We should not be surprised, then, to learn that television is also one of the leading causes of sleep disturbances in children. For instance, one important study published in *Pediatrics*,[9] the peer-reviewed scientific journal of the American Academy of Pediatrics, found a significant rise in sleep disturbances in children who watched television at bedtime. An even greater frequency of problems was documented in children who had a television in their own bedroom. Some misguided parents allow their children to use television as a kind of "sleep aid," permitting them to fall asleep, exhausted, in front of the television set. Ironically, falling asleep in front of the television was found to be associated with the highest number of sleep disturbances.

One of the many negative effects of watching television at night is that it delays bedtime, thus robbing your child of crucial time that would normally be spent sleeping. Many children, quite understandably, will resist bedtime just so they can watch a particular program or, in many cases, so that they can watch *any* program. Children seem especially susceptible to the industry message that if you are not watching television you are missing something important.

Watching television during the day is also likely to cause sleep disturbances by robbing your child of time that would otherwise be devoted to physical activities, such as playing outside in the fresh air and sunshine and engaging in healthy exercise. By passively watching television, a child is failing to get the exercise needed to ensure a good night's sleep. Furthermore, violent or otherwise exciting and stimulating programs may result in your child becoming anxious and therefore having difficulty falling asleep or experiencing night wakings. The negative consequences of inadequate sleep on school performance and on health are too great to ignore.

Infants and younger children cannot watch television intelligently. They cannot distinguish between reality and fantasy as presented on television. As a result, they may appear outwardly calm, but inside, children can become very agitated and emotionally distraught. Even seemingly calm and happy television programs can have the same negative effects. Bad dreams and fragmented sleep are common consequences of watching television at bedtime.

There has also been serious concern recently about the apparently detrimental effects on children's health of the electromagnetic radiation generated by television sets. We have all observed that children who watch television, especially at night, are agitated, enervated, and hyperactive. They seem drugged. Not surprisingly, studies have demonstrated that nighttime exposure to a low-frequency electromagnetic field, such as that generated by a television set, is associated with reduced total sleep time, impaired sleep efficiency, reduced periods of Stages III and IV slow-wave sleep, and reduced periods of slow-wave activity.[10] These disruptions are caused entirely by the radiation associated with a television rather than by program content, though this should not be interpreted to mean that program content does not have an effect on children's sleep. Studies also show that exposure to intermittent 60 hertz magnetic fields, such as that created by cellular telephones, disrupts the action of neuronal and cardiovascular reflexes, including those involved in the control of temperature, blood pressure, and respiration, resulting in heart rate variability.[11] A modern television emits about the same level of radiation. Surely this sort of exposure on a regular basis cannot be good for our children's sleep.

There are many other very good reasons to avoid television. Residential or occupational exposures to electromagnetic fields have been reported to be associated with health problems, particularly cancer and reproductive mishaps. Some people doubt the accuracy of these scientific findings, but they owe it to their children to err on the side of caution. Specifically, studies have linked exposure to low levels of electromagnetic radiation from household appliances such as televisions, video monitors, and electric blankets to the development of acute lymphoblastic leukemia in children.[12–15] The risk of developing this devastating disease was increased with children's use of electric blankets or mattress pads and three other electrical appliances (hair dryers, video machines in arcades, and video games connected to a television). Risks rose with increasing number of hours per day children spent watching television, but, interestingly enough, the risks were similar regardless of the usual distance that children maintained from the television. Other studies have detected carcinogenic changes in human cells as a result of exposure to the electromagnetic radiation of color television, personal computers, cellular telephones, and microwave ovens,[16] all of which are commonly found in the home.

Even if these studies do not sway you, bear in mind that those truly valuable television programs, such as nature shows, that are broadcast in the evenings and at bedtime, can be videotaped and viewed at a more opportune time. There is no reason why a child should lose any sleep because of a television program.

Out of growing concern over the rise in television-related health problems in children, in 1999 the American Academy of Pediatrics Committee on Public Education issued a set of recommendations aimed at promoting responsible use of television and other electronic media. One important recommendation that the Academy made states:

> Pediatricians should urge parents to avoid television viewing for children under the age of two years. Although certain television programs may be promoted to this age group, research on early brain development shows that babies and toddlers have a critical need for direct interactions with parents and other significant care givers (e.g., child care providers) for healthy brain growth and the development of appropriate social, emotional, and cognitive skills. Therefore, exposing such young children to television programs should be discouraged.[17]

These recommendations are laudatory as far as they go, but I think we would all agree that the benefits of avoiding television should not be limited to children under two years. The brains of children past the age of two are just as much in a state of development. The longer parents can protect their children from television, the more opportunities children will have to develop social, emotional, and cognitive skills. After all, success in life is not dependent on the ability to sit passively in front of a television: It is dependent on the development and exercise of social, emotional, and cognitive skills.

I would also like to suggest that it is inappropriate and counterproductive for a child to have a television set in his bedroom. The temptation to watch television past bedtime or before bedtime is too great. It is also too tempting for parents to ignore their children and just let the television baby-sit the child. This is never a good idea. The American Academy of Pediatrics report that I quoted above supports this position, urging that parents should create "an 'electronic media-free' environment in children's rooms" and avoid the "use of media as an electronic baby-sitter." Your child's bedroom should be a sanctuary from all the distractions of life. A television has the undesirable effect of changing a child's bedroom from a realm of calm and rest into a den of noise, stress, and distraction. Television does not give anyone the feeling of being safe and secure, which is the way we want to feel when we fall asleep.

Instead of a television, fill your child's room with books and appropriate magazines. Let the period between dinner and bedtime be a quiet time of reading, conversation, or gentle, intellect-stimulating games, such as card games or chess. Card games foster problem-solving abilities and have the added benefit of strengthening social bonds. I remember with great fondness playing card games in the evening with my grandmother. I loved the genteel and sociable atmosphere she brought to the game. Even as a little boy, I also appreciated how beautiful it was that she was teaching me games she had played with her own grandmother when she was my age. The sense of family continuity was very precious to me. It will be for your child as well.

When you play card games—or any games that require thinking, problem solving, planning, and observation—with your child, you are helping her to develop valuable cognitive skills. Your child will learn to formulate long-term strategies and problem-solving abilities that will keep her in good stead her entire life. Unlike television, genteel games exercise the brain but do not enervate the mind or body. After a good parlor game, your child will be able to sleep in a state of mental satisfaction and relaxation, untroubled by mental disturbances.

Avoiding Video or Computer Games

Everything I have said about television holds true for video games, computer games, or anything of a similar nature. I include in this category anything like a computer game: Nintendo, Atari, PlayStation, Game Boy, and so on. It is especially worrying that so many computer games marketed to children are violent. It cannot be acceptable in a civilized society for children to play games that reward them for killing or committing mayhem. I am not prepared to say that the dramatic rise in the level of violent killings perpetrated by children and teenagers in the United States in recent years is entirely due to computer games, but I think we can all agree that any game or activity that legitimizes murder sends the wrong message to our children.

Although there are perfectly harmless, nonviolent, and perhaps even mildly educational computer games, even these should be avoided at bedtime. The time that your child spends staring into a computer screen playing a game is time wasted. It is a mistake to imagine that computer games "hone skills," "improve hand-eye coordination," or stimulate the mind. Like television, they stultify and deaden the mind. They replace thought and intelligence with numbness and mental torpor. Computer games do not enlighten: They suppress the development of cognitive abilities. Surely, no reasonable parents would want this for their child.

Children need and crave mental stimulation, and if they do not get it from their parents, relatives, neighbors, friends, or other loved ones, they may seek it from computer games or other flashy and attractive lures. This is exactly analogous to food. All humans crave nourishment, and if we are unable to satisfy our craving with wholesome and nutritious food, we can easily be misled into satisfying it with surrogate food, namely junk food, which has a superficial resemblance to real food but has no inherent nutritional value and is usually unhealthy. Computer games are an un-healthy substitute for real human interaction. Children need to interact with adults. Their intellect, emotions, imagination, creativity, spirit, rea-son, and humor all need to be stimulated. The best way to achieve this is through social interaction, that is, by making your child part of a vibrant human community.

Books are a beautiful complement to human interaction because they too stimulate the imagination and expand your child's mind. Com-puter games cannot achieve this, and, I suspect that, with long-term expo-sure, they hinder mental development, if for no other reason than that they take up valuable time that would be better spent interacting with liv-ing human beings or in solitary, creative play.

Some of the best toys and games for children, especially ones that are appropriate for that special period between dinner and bedtime, are the old standard creative toys that parents have been giving children for ages. Younger children love playing with building blocks. Older children may find enjoyment in construction toys, such as Legos, or other toys that enable a child to build according to his fancy. Some children love "play-ing house," using toy tea sets. Both boys and girls love playing with stuffed animals, dolls, and action figures. Any sort of toy that permits your child to be creative, imaginative, and nonviolent is appropriate for the period before bed.

In short, have your child completely avoid computer games at bed-time. Although it is unacceptable for a child to have a television in the bed-room, I suppose there is little I can say to persuade most modern parents to avoid placing a computer there. Just ensure that the computer is not used for games and is just a tool for homework or other creative activities.

Avoiding Conflicts

Before bedtime and at bedtime, avoid fighting with your child or with any-one else in the house. Children are emotional creatures. They are much more affected by the negative emotions aroused by conflicts than are adults.

Adults may brood longer, but children are more deeply affected by emotional disturbances. Children rarely comprehend the reason for fights. They only experience terror, hurt, and a sense of insecurity. None of these feelings is conducive to sleep.

To illustrate the importance of this, let me tell you about Barbara and her family. One warm summer evening, Barbara served her family and guests a lovely dinner outside on the terrace. Her eldest son, Oliver, then age seven, had been in a very good mood all day and had eaten heartily at dinner, but his exuberant spirits, inspired perhaps by the presence of guests and aggravated by the late hour, had a slight manic edge. It was clear that poor Oliver was tired and was pushing himself beyond his endurance. He was being allowed to stay up to be with the guests, but it was really too late for him.

Barbara had prepared a lovely dessert of fresh berries picked from her garden. There were just enough berries to fill each person's plate, but no more. Oliver, without thinking, impetuously grabbed the bowl the moment it was placed on the table and served himself an enormous helping. His father calmly commented on this and asked Oliver to spoon half of the berries on his plate back into the bowl. Suddenly, Oliver's mood shifted. The irritability and crankiness that he had been suppressing were unleashed, and he refused to give up any of the berries. His father, unwisely, reacted with anger and ordered him from the table. With a burst of anger, Oliver refused. His father then aggressively stood up, as if to threaten Oliver. It was a terrible way to handle a tired child, who could not really be held accountable for his actions. Oliver screamed in rage and fear. He jumped up and ran from the table and into the house. He was very upset. His extreme fatigue had caused his usual good judgment to be suspended. This bright child, who was normally graced with perfect manners, was simply unable to manage his fatigue rationally and recognize that he was not quite himself. This is perfectly understandable. He was just a child. His father, I should add, was to be faulted for not handling the situation with the understanding, compassion, and grace required.

Oliver ran into the house, up the stairs, into his bedroom, and flung himself on top of his bed. He was enraged and exhausted. Alone, and feeling awful, Oliver cried himself to sleep. His mother came in later, undressed him, and slipped him under the covers. His face was still red, contorted, and stained with tears.

Unfortunately, the unpleasant emotions that coursed through his mind and body did not simply evaporate when he fell asleep. Oliver was still upset. He tossed and turned in his troubled sleep. The stress of the conflict at the dinner table had not been resolved but had been building through the night. Then around midnight, his body could take no more of the mounting stress, and he sat bolt upright in bed and vomited profusely. His mother came in the room, washed him off, cleaned up the mess, changed the bedclothes, and held him lovingly in her arms until he fell back asleep. Her gentleness resolved the problem, and Oliver was able to sleep through the night.

The next day, Barbara and her husband discussed the implications of the event and resolved never again to react in anger toward their children, especially in the evening. They recognized that, as the adults, it was their responsibility to act compassionately, rationally, and gracefully at all times, but especially when their children were not themselves, which is common at the end of the day.

Now, if you find that you regularly have to battle with your children to get them to go to bed, you will already have learned that battling does not help. Rationally determine why your child resists going to bed. Is it because your child is simply not sleepy at the prescribed bedtime? Is it because you have neglected to provide your child with pleasant bedtime rituals? Is it because your child just wants to spend more time with you? Whatever the cause of the problem, identify it and solve it. Bedtime should be the most peaceful and relaxing time of day.

Sometimes, random emotional upsets can occur at bedtime. These may be related to stress your child is under from school, disturbances that occurred during the day, or just crankiness from exhaustion. Crankiness is better ignored. It is up to you as the responsible adult to have the wisdom to know when to ignore undesirable behavior rather than drawing attention to it. If your child is upset or uncooperative because of stress incurred during the day, sit down with your child and discuss the problem. Solve the problem as best you can or reassure your child that a good night's sleep will be part of the solution. Children may not always be able to articulate or convey their problems to you in a way that you can understand or appreciate. The best thing you can do, however, is to listen, be supportive, and let your child know by your presence, touch, and gentleness that he can depend on you. It is best that you do not add to your child's frustration by becoming frustrated yourself. Be wise and compassionate with your child. While letting your child know that bad behavior is not acceptable, have the wisdom to overlook it and to reward good behavior.

Avoiding Eating Just Before Bedtime

It is best for digestion, and therefore for sleep, that your child refrain from eating immediately before going to bed, whenever possible. Set your dinnertime early enough so that there is at least a good hour between the end of dinner and bedtime. Food requires time to digest. While sleeping, however, digestion does not progress in the same way it does when we are awake. It slows and even stops. The result is gas, cramps, and stomach pain. None of these conditions permits restful sleep.

We should not, however, confuse eating with breast-feeding. Breast-feeding has the wonderful benefit of promoting sleep. Babies and young children who are still nursing should be allowed to nurse as often as they want before going to bed and during the night. Newborn babies may nurse as often as several times an hour in any given twenty-four-hour period. In fact, an eight-week-old infant obtains approximately 30 percent of all food volume in the hours between midnight and 8 A.M. Nothing must interfere with this vital process of infant nourishment. When your child is old enough to have weaned herself off mother's milk, you can set your dinnertime to an appropriate hour that is sufficiently far from bedtime so that your child has time to digest, but also close enough to bedtime so that your child does not grow hungry and require nourishment.

I should like to emphasize that the advice to avoid food just before bedtime is not about restricting, regulating, or monitoring your child's eating patterns with the aim of "training" him to sleep through the night. It is simply about acknowledging and working with the digestive rhythms of the body. Attempts to control children's sleep patterns by restricting food are counterintuitive and useless. Children do not need to be "controlled" by their parents. They need and want to be incorporated into family life and appreciated for the unique creatures they are. Infants and children are not adults. They should not, therefore, be expected to display the same sleeping or eating patterns as adults. Trying to force children to adapt to an adult sleeping schedule or a schedule that is more convenient for adults is unrealistic and can only bring misery and conflict. Although all parents would like their children to get a good night's sleep, the idea that you can engineer this by controlling your child's food intake is both mistaken and ineffective.

Unfortunately, in the United States, these alarmingly misguided ideas have gained a measure of currency in recent years. Concerned healthcare professionals, however, have repeatedly warned that these ideas and practices are extremely dangerous to children. Informed doctors and hospitals have become deeply distressed at the increasing numbers of babies and young children who have been rushed into the hospital because of severe malnourishment and failure to thrive, all because their parents restricted the child's food intake under the mistaken belief that food restriction was an appropriate way to "train" children to sleep through the night.

In response to this worrying situation, the District IV Chapter Convention of the American Academy of Pediatrics passed a resolution (#22T) calling on the American Academy of Pediatrics to "investigate the infant management program outlined in *Preparation for Parenting* and *On Becoming BABYWISE* and determine the extent of its potentially harmful effects on infant health and resolved that the American Academy of Pediatrics alert its members, other organizations, and parents of its findings and inform healthcare providers how to discern when the program is in use and how to facilitate patient care while on the program." Among other professional medical responses to these problems, Dr. Matthew Aney, a California pediatrician, published an editorial in *AAP News* (the monthly medical news magazine for members of the American Academy of Pediatrics) in which he discussed having personally reviewed dozens of medical records of infants with health problems ranging from low weight gain to dehydration to symptoms of depression that developed after parents had followed the bad feeding advice contained in these books.[18] Following the advice in these books, parents had restricted their children's food intake under the mistaken belief that this would "train" their children to sleep through the night.

If parents would listen to their own intuition, they would instantly recognize bad advice for what it is. Parents who use good sense will know instinctively to protect their child from any system that advocates withholding food, instituting feeding schedules, inflicting corporal punishment to any degree, ignoring a child's cries, or anything that causes a baby any degree of discomfort or distress. A baby may be unable to verbalize her needs, but all babies instinctively know what their needs are, and they will cry when any of those needs are not being met. Indeed, as the American Academy of Pediatrics' "Statement on Breastfeeding and the Use of Human Milk" states:

> Newborns should be nursed whenever they show signs of hunger, such as increased alertness or activity, mouthing, or rooting. Crying is a *late* indicator of hunger.[19]

Crying, then, occurs only when a baby's noncrying attempts at communicating its hunger have been ignored. The notion that a baby "deviously" uses its crying to "manipulate" parents is deeply mistaken, to say the very least.

Scientific childcare experts agree that the best "feeding schedules" are ones babies design themselves. Scheduled feedings designed by parents may put babies at risk for poor weight gain and dehydration. An infant's physiological need to nurse several times during the night requires that the infant awaken and nurse. If the mother is not sleeping with the baby and he cannot find the breast, he will cry to alert the mother to pick him up and nurse him. Ignoring the infant's cries will not "teach" him anything because the baby is not responding to an intellectual need but rather to a physiological need for nourishment. As your baby grows older, his need to nurse during the night will diminish on its own.

By five to six months of age, most babies will have developed beyond the need for continuous nourishment. Nighttime awakenings are not always an indication that your child is hungry, thirsty, or nutritionally deprived. If your older baby is properly nourished during daytime breast-feedings, nighttime awakenings will rarely be in response to hunger.

Breast-feeding may not be the most precise word to describe night-time feedings, for rarely at this age does the baby awaken out of a physiological need for increased calories. Babies at this stage of development may awaken for a gentle kiss on the nipple, reminding the mother that the baby is hers and that he is there with her. Breast-feeding mothers of babies of all ages have reported to me that they find that the suckle in the middle of the night is quite distinct from the suckle associated with the first feeding of the morning when baby is hungry. Even though this need for comfort is not necessarily related to a need for calories, it is just as important to satisfy. One can keep a baby continuously fed to satiety, but if his psychological and emotional needs are not being met, you will not have a happy or healthy baby.

I might add that it is never a good idea to put your baby to bed with a bottle propped up, no matter what you put in the bottle. Babies should always be held during feedings and *never* left alone with a bottle in the crib. This is only asking for trouble. Your baby may spit up or choke on the fluid and may be unable to turn away from the propped bottle. Too much apple juice, formula, or cow's milk during nighttime feedings may cause wide variations in the baby's blood sugar. At first, the ingestion of these fluids may have a calming effect, but soon thereafter they will be stimulating and irritating, causing sleep disturbances.

Now that we have clarified the issue, let me say again that, for the older child—one that has been entirely weaned from mother's milk—eating just before bed has the same disadvantages as it does for adults: It can induce gastric distress and intestinal disturbances and can set up an unhealthy psychological dependency. For better sleep, then, plan your evening meal at an appropriate time before bedtime.

Avoiding Bright Lights at Nighttime

Although the modern world has developed technologies that can blur the natural distinction between day and night, our body and all of our bodily systems, especially our endocrine system, remain firmly rooted in our evolutionary past. Quite simply, we are dependent for our health on the natural conditions that prevailed when humans lived in the wild. Our endocrine system, for instance, is dependent on the regular, natural alteration between the hours of daylight and the hours of darkness. Without adequate exposure to sunlight and adequate exposure to darkness, our bodily systems cannot function properly.

It is a testament to our ingenuity that we humans have figured out ways to extend the hours of daylight by the use of electric lights, but, in so doing, we are disrupting our internal clock and, hence, our sleep. Children may not be more susceptible to the disruptions caused by artificial light during normal nighttime hours, but they are more likely to express their internal discomfort through crankiness. Studies show that exposure to bright light during the early hours of darkness delays the nocturnal melatonin peak and alters cortisol, growth hormone, prolactin, and nocturnal vasopressin secretion.[20] Even the amount of light that is equivalent to a 100-watt lightbulb held ten feet away is sufficiently powerful to disorder our internal clock and disrupt sleep patterns.[21] It is interesting that this disruption of the internal clock caused by artificial lights at nighttime is a modern phenomenon. The light of candles, fire, and oil lamps is not bright enough to affect the internal clock.

Although it is probably unrealistic today to live without the benefit of artificial lights to illuminate our seemingly necessary nighttime activities, you can minimize the negative effects on your children of artificial light during nighttime hours by keeping lights as low as possible in the evening. Better yet, organize your day so that most activities will be completed by nightfall. You and your child can then spend the evening hours quietly and peacefully preparing for bed. It is not possible to work against our hormones and our internal clock, so it makes more sense to work with them to guarantee a good night's sleep.

Avoiding Circumcision

Many American parents and doctors once used to assume, automatically, that circumcision was a good thing. New scientific studies, however, have revealed important information that parents will find extremely useful. We now know, for example, that there are many good reasons for protecting your newborn son from circumcision. Preventing the inevitable sleep disturbances caused by this operation is one of these reasons, and it is one with which many parents may be unfamiliar.

We all have to admit, first, that the topic of circumcision can be very upsetting for many people. Even some doctors can get defensive when the issue is raised. It seems that everyone has a strong opinion on the issue of routine circumcision. Actually, most of what people think they know is outdated and inaccurate. There is so much ignorance about the medical facts of circumcision that most American parents are very surprised to learn that the United States is the only Western country where routine neonatal circumcision is commonplace. In Europe, for instance, it is unheard of.

As a doctor who has carefully reviewed *all* of the medical literature on this subject, I can assure you that there are no legitimate medical reasons for routinely circumcising babies. Likewise, I believe there are no legitimate social reasons for circumcising babies. These days, an increasing number of American families agree. In large parts of America today, the majority of boys have intact penises. The rate of routine nonreligious newborn circumcision is falling so fast that, within a few short decades, I predict that most of America will have re-embraced the time-honored American tradition of leaving boys intact (uncircumcised). Even the idea of circumcision as a religious rite, as in Muslim and Jewish culture, is being rethought within those communities. I think, however, that it would be helpful to address some of the most common concerns that some parents still have about circumcision so that they can confidently make a decision that is fair to their babies.

One of the biggest anxieties that parents have is the issue of a baby looking like his father. I can assure you that circumcising a baby does not make him look like his circumcised father, nor does it create a "bond" between father and son. Bonds are created by the expression of love, not by cutting the penis. Little boys do not care whether their father's penis was circumcised or not. They just want their fathers to love them.

I find that fathers who were born during the days of the Cold War–era phenomenon of mass circumcision are very interested to learn that the foreskin is an integral part of the penis. Simply put: It is supposed to be there. Otherwise, it wouldn't be there. Additionally, the foreskin has many very useful, protective, and sensory functions. Fascinating scientific research has now proven that the foreskin is the most richly sensitive part of the penis.[22–24] Of course, males can get along with a reduced level of penile sensitivity, but it seems unfair to deny them any choice over such a deeply personal and private part of their body.

Fathers are also keenly interested to learn that circumcision results in the loss of at least 50 percent of the skin of the penis, much of which, in most infants and children, extends well beyond the glans. Sometimes, the foreskin represents over half the length of the penis. I hardly think that any male could remain indifferent about circumcision when he realizes that it shortens and desensitizes the penis. It is my experience that when the average father learns this information, he is usually very eager to protect his newborn son from circumcision.

Another thing that parents should bear in mind is that it simply does not make sense to operate on a healthy baby. We can justify performing operations in the neonatal period in response to genuine diseases, injuries, or deformities, but neonatal circumcision is not performed in response to a genuine medical problem. It is a surgery that, illogically, is performed on a perfectly healthy body part.

Now, I am afraid that I must inform you that there is no debate that circumcising the penis is extremely traumatic and stressful for baby boys. This fact has been extensively documented in the medical literature.[25] Infants have a limited capacity to distance or protect themselves from stress. They cannot run away or defend themselves. Instead, they respond to stress by crying or, in extreme situations, by withdrawing psychologically. They appear to be asleep, but actually they are in a semicomatose state that is very different from sleep. This state is characterized by a decrease of REM sleep, where the arousal continuum is at a low point, where thresholds to sensory stimulation are high, and where motor activity is low.[26] Normally, infants begin their sleep cycle with REM sleep, but after enduring the stress of being circumcised, infants experience prolonged non-REM sleep.

Studies conducted at the Institute of Child Development at the University of Minnesota,[27,28] the Albert Einstein College of Medicine,[29] and the University of Colorado School of Medicine[30] reveal that circumcised infants suffer from a detrimental shift in sleep pattern, staying awake for longer periods of time than they did before the surgery. Even when they are able to sleep, the amount of shallow sleep increases, and the crucial periods of deep sleep decrease. To try to calm themselves and ease the pain emanating from the surgical wound, circumcised babies suck harder, faster, and more vigorously at their bottles, making them less available to their environment and less able to interact with their mother.[31,32]

An invaluable study from Georgetown University Medical School also showed that when male infants who underwent circumcision were compared to female infants (who are not circumcised in the United States), as well as to genitally intact male infants, the circumcised infants suffered from deprivation of active sleep time. They spent more time awake, they spent more time agitated, and they took longer to fall asleep.[33] Not surprisingly, they cried more and experienced a greater drop in heart rate. Undoubtedly, these effects are related to the stress of the surgery as well as the throbbing postoperative pain, which may last for weeks because of the long time it takes such a large surgical wound to heal.

These negative behavior changes are related to changes in cortisol levels.[34] In addition to its role in sleep, cortisol is a stress hormone. Beyond crying and displaying agitation, babies cannot articulate the distress and pain they are experiencing. Cortisol levels, however, clearly indicate the amount of distress that babies are suffering. A very important study conducted at the Institute of Child Development at the University of Minnesota found that babies who suffered the most distress during circumcision exhibited large cortisol rises thirty minutes and ninety minutes after the surgery.[35]

Disruptions in the cycle of cortisol release are only part of the reason that circumcision leads to sleep problems in infants. Even when circumcision is performed with anesthesia, studies consistently show that cortisol levels, blood pressure, and oxygen saturation rise dramatically, beyond the level that any baby would normally ever experience.[36-39] It may be possible to *reduce* the pain of the surgery to a small extent, but the body knows when it has sustained a wound and it reacts accordingly. Rises in cortisol levels, whether accompanied by detectable pain or not, cause internal distress and necessarily disrupt sleep.

Medical science has still not documented all of the negative consequences of circumcision, the most obvious of which is a permanent loss of a normal, protective, and sensitive part of the penis—a fact that has been confirmed by many independent, classic studies, some of which were conducted at the University of Manitoba[40] and the famed Mayo Clinic in Rochester, Minnesota.[41] One of the long-term effects of circumcision that has been documented includes a lowered threshold to pain.[42,43] It seems that the pain of circumcision results in neurological changes that cause babies to display more frenzied reactions to painful stimuli. In other words, circumcised babies feel pain more acutely than either genitally intact baby boys or female babies. Independent studies conducted at Washington University School of Medicine,[44] the University of California at San Diego School of Medicine,[45] and the University of Rochester School of Medicine[46] have confirmed that circumcision can also lead to a disruption of breast-feeding and an impairment of infant/maternal attachment.[47]

Circumcision causes severe short-term sleep problems. Can these problems extend into the long term? One highly suggestive study, conducted at Northwestern University Medical School in Chicago and published in 1984, provides tantalizing clues. The study found that among four- to eight-month-old infants from middle-class American families, the problem of night waking was significantly greater among boys than among girls. Now, we must remember that this study was conducted at the height of the campaign for mass routine circumcision. Therefore, we can safely assume that the vast majority of the male babies in this study had been subjected to circumcision. It is important to note that these boys did not suffer from any other sleep problems, such as snoring or mouth breathing, which could account for the difference. Likewise, the method of feeding did not affect the reported sleep problems.[48] Other studies have found similar results.[49] We owe it to ourselves and to our precious children to consider the possibility that circumcision is to blame for the increase in long-term sleep disorders among the male babies in this study.

These are the sad facts that have been demonstrated by rigorous, objective scientific investigation. Parents have a right to know this information. I honestly believe that parents instinctively want to protect their babies from harm. I am also convinced that only the most extraordinary and persistent pressures and scare tactics can subvert a mother and father's natural impulse to protect their baby from stress. We should learn to respect and admire God's design for the body. We must learn to respect our sons for who they are, rather than try to transform them surgically into what someone else has pressured us into thinking they should be.

Jewish families who find themselves in a conflict over the desire to protect their baby and the desire to respect their religion will find great comfort in Dr. Ronald Goldman's thoughtful book *Questioning Circumcision: A Jewish Perspective,*[50] which has an excellent foreword by Rabbi Raymond Singer. Whatever your feelings on the issue, reading this book will open up new avenues of thought. It performs a great service to Jewish families because it opens a welcome and long overdue discussion that will ultimately benefit and strengthen the Jewish community.

Finally, let me remind you of the latest scientific findings that circumcising your baby boy's penis does not prevent infections, cancer, sexually transmitted diseases, or make the penis cleaner or easier to keep clean. As I have written elsewhere,[51] cutting off the foreskin is like cutting off the eyelids. The surgically and artificially externalized glans of the circumcised penis is much more exposed to dirt if the protective foreskin that normally shields it is amputated. Similarly, the eyes would be more exposed to dirt if the eyelids were amputated.

Circumcision cannot guarantee that your son will grow up to be a healthy, responsible, loving, caring, respectful, reverent, law-abiding citizen.

Neither does it protect him from the consequences of poor decisions he may make in the future. Only good parenting and education guide your son in the direction of these worthy goals. Cherishing your baby boy for the miracle that he is, respecting his right to bodily sovereignty, and protecting him from surgical trauma will not only be good for his health and your peace of mind, but it will be good for his sleep.

Avoiding Caffeine

The consumption of coffee in our society has gone from fad, to ritual, to social custom, to a form of self-medication. Caffeine is the most widely used psychoactive substance and is properly recognized as a drug of abuse. We all know people who seem to be unable to wake up without first drinking a cup of coffee in the morning. They are not drinking it for the pleasure they get in its taste or its warmth, but for the stimulating effects that the caffeine in the coffee has on their brain. Caffeine consumption leads to increased arousal and hypothalamic-pituitary-adrenal axis activation. As such, caffeine can prevent us from falling asleep at night.

Few parents would give their children coffee or tea to drink, and for this reason they may assume that their children are safe from the sleep-disrupting properties of caffeine, but the large amount of caffeine that the average American child does consume from other, more hidden sources provides reason for concern, especially in relation to its effects on sleep.

The amount of caffeine in a cup of coffee ranges from 100 to 175 milligrams. A twelve-ounce glass of iced tea contains 70 milligrams. According to documents prepared by the National Soft Drink Association and the U.S. Food and Drug Administration, the amount of caffeine in a twelve-ounce can of Coca-Cola is 45.6 milligrams.[52] Diet Coke has the same amount.

Caffeine is even put in popular "fruit drinks," which actually contain very little fruit juice, such as Sunkist Orange drink, which contains an unbelievable 40 milligrams of caffeine in every twelve-ounce can. Not only is caffeine found in great amounts in "cola" drinks but also in even higher concentrations in colorless soft drinks that are marketed as "energy boosters," such as Jolt (71.2 milligrams), Mountain Dew (55 milligrams), and Surge (51 milligrams). Even health food stores are selling a new, faddish soft drink, often marketed to children, made from the Amazonian guarana berry, which is claimed to be two and a half times stronger than the caffeine found in coffee, soft drinks, and tea. This is a type of stimulation that our children do not need.

Caffeine is found in high concentrations in chocolate as well. Hot cocoa, prepared from commercial instant mixes, contains 4 milligrams/ serving of caffeine, as well as 62 milligrams/serving of theobromine, another psychoactive drug in the same family as caffeine and cocaine. Instant cold chocolate milk mixes contain an average of 5 milligrams per serving of caffeine and 58 milligrams per serving of theobromine.[53] Chocolate may have less caffeine than cola drinks, but even the amount found in chocolate can have noticeable effects on a child's behavior and sleep patterns.

Caffeine should be a major concern to parents because it can cause mood swings, irritability, and headaches. In terms of headaches, a vicious cycle is set up by caffeine. Not only does caffeine cause headaches that in turn cause sleep disturbances, but studies show that the sleep deficit caused by caffeine-induced headaches will cause additional headaches, leading to more sleep disturbances.[54] Additionally, caffeine consumption can induce panic attacks.[55] Part of the reason that caffeine disrupts sleep is that it suppresses melatonin secretion at night and attenuates the normal drop in body temperature associated with normal sleep. These negative effects of caffeine, interestingly enough, are magnified when combined with exposure to bright lights during the normal hours of darkness.[56]

A very interesting study of American children between the ages of eleven and fourteen found that boys consumed significantly more caffeinated beverages than girls and that caffeine intake was significantly related to self-reported sleep disorders as well as daytime sleepiness and difficulty in waking up in the morning.[57]

Bearing all this in mind, you will do your child and yourself an enormous favor if you strive to eliminate caffeine from your child's diet. The price your child pays in terms of lost sleep, impaired nutrition, and health disturbances is not worth the false pleasure derived from the products that contain caffeine. Instead of caffeinated beverages, treat your children to pure, fresh, and naturally delicious fruit juices. If your child wants something warm to drink, instead of hot cocoa, offer a soothing cup of hot apple cider. Good health and good sleep are the natural results of avoiding inferior products of the factory and exploring the wide and rewarding world of real foods.

Avoiding Over-the-Counter Cold Medications

If your child is suffering from a cold, avoid the temptation to give him any sort of over-the-counter medications. Such medications include cough-suppressants, decongestants, and antihistamines. Many of these products contain alcohol, but even if they are alcohol-free, they will contain powerful drugs that can seriously disrupt your child's sleep. Many of these drugs cause sleepiness during the day.[58] The other negative effect of these drugs is that, by suppressing the symptoms of a cold, they can prolong the cold.

Many parents are aware of the need to give their children vitamin C instead. The benefits of vitamin C are too well known for me to list them here. Some patients, however, have reported that large doses of vitamin C can induce insomnia and fragmented sleep, although this has not yet been verified by case-controlled studies.

The other regrettable and well-documented side effect of vitamin C, when taken in large doses, is soft, loose stools.[59,60] Being frequently awakened in the middle of the night by the need to go to the bathroom is, as you can well imagine, a major inconvenience and a cause of poor sleep. If your child is taking vitamin C, give it to her in the morning and at noon only. Avoid giving it in the evening, and if loose stools and an unusually frequent need to evacuate result, decrease the dosage of vitamin C until you find the maximum amount that your child can take and still maintain normal bowel control.

In short, avoid anything that tends to upset your child's mind or body. Cherish your children for the miracle they are. Make them feel safe and secure, and let them know that you are completely dependable and trustworthy. Remember that their goodness does not depend on their ability to adapt to an adult schedule. Children are inherently good and loving. Depending on their age and stage of development, children have needs, requirements, and rhythms that are different from those of adults. Learn to recognize these unique needs and work with them rather than against them. By trusting your instincts to protect and cherish your child, by avoiding all the things that bring turmoil, confusion, and distress to your child, you will be laying the foundation for a good night's sleep for both you and your child.

Chapter 4

Bedroom Hygiene: Making Your Child's Bedroom Just Right

*H*aving a bedroom that is conducive to good sleep is important for all of us. Even animals in the wild take great care in selecting the spot where they will bed down for the night. Gorillas, for example, very carefully spend several hours every evening choosing the right branches in the right tree in the right corner of the forest to make their nest. The room in which your child sleeps should be arranged with just as much care, if not more.

Even if your child sleeps with you in your bed, I think it is nice if your child can have his own bedroom too, circumstances permitting. Like teenagers and adults, children need a space that they can call their own. From a practical standpoint, they need a place where they can store, organize, and play with their possessions. They need a place where they can freely entertain their friends without infringing on the privacy of other members of the household. Children, like all of us, need a private space where they can be alone, where they can "recharge their batteries," and where they can renew their spirits. Just as we hope that our own need for solitude will be respected, so we should respect our child's need for solitude.

An infant, however, has probably not developed this need and will benefit by spending all of her time in the company of others. For this reason, I think it is important that infants should sleep with their parents, ideally in the same bed but, depending on the circumstances, in a bassinet placed immediately next to the parent's bed so that the mother can easily transfer the baby to the mother's bed during the night for nursing and cuddling. Of course, there may be legitimate circumstances that make the goal of sleeping in the same bed or even in the same room with your baby unachievable, and, if this is the case, you will have to develop suitable strategies for meeting your baby's nocturnal needs with efficiency.

In general, the room in which your child sleeps should be clean, neat, well ventilated, orderly, and quiet. When the lights are extinguished and the curtains are closed, the room should be dark. These rules pertain to the child's own bedroom, even if he actually sleeps with you, and they pertain equally to your bedroom if your child sleeps with you. As soon as the child is old enough, in partnership with your child, furnish and decorate your child's room according to his tastes, pleasures, and delights rather than to anyone else's ideas about what is appropriate or traditional for children. Obviously, a child's room should be free of paintings or objects that might cause fear or discomfort. Many children, for instance, are frightened by clowns, with their garish and sometimes ghoulish makeup. Remember that a child needs to feel safe and secure and does not need the stress of waking up and seeing a distressing or nightmarish object.

Another important thing to remember is that the room in which your child sleeps should be kept spotlessly clean. Carpets and rugs should be regularly vacuumed and washed. Bare floorboards should be washed regularly. All furniture surfaces should regularly be wiped clean with a damp cloth and kept free of dust. A room that is not clean will be a fertile feeding and breeding ground for rodents and insects of all sizes and descriptions. A dirty room will also provide a virulent breeding ground for harmful molds, bacteria, and microscopic spider mites whose excrement can cause allergic responses and respiratory disease.

Still, this said, one should not become obsessive and unreasonable about the order in which your child wants to keep her room. Allow your child to design her own space as long as the room remains tasteful, practical, clean, and free of dust.

As we all know, a *sterile* environment is neither achievable nor desirable. Our natural world is home to countless invisible microscopic bacterial species, the vast majority of which are either harmless or actually beneficial. One of the primary objects in keeping your child's room clean is to eliminate the common allergens, such as insect and spider mite feces, that can cause problems with the skin and with breathing.

Eliminating mites, fleas, ticks, spiders, flies, silverfish, cockroaches, worms, and other undesirable and bothersome pests from the bedroom is also very important. These creatures are attracted to dirt, dust, and dander. If you have pets in your house, you will need to redouble your housekeeping efforts.

Parents know that keeping a child's room clean and orderly is a full-time job, but it is a job that ought to be done with your child's health in mind. It need not become a cause for daily battles, as long as you approach it with the right frame of mind. Make the attainment of cleanliness and neatness a goal for both you and your child. From babyhood on, you can make the daily cleaning and straightening up of your child's room one of the activities you share with your child. You and your child will cherish the time spent together. The valuable example you will be setting for your child will instill in him the importance of cleanliness and neatness. When your child is older, he will automatically keep his room tidy because having a tidy room will make him more comfortable.

Children's rooms should also be free of any and all electronic devices, or anything that emits electromagnetic radiation. This includes televisions, computers, mobile telephones, and so forth. Studies show that an electromagnetic field of only 50 hertz can impair sleep.[1] (I discuss this point in greater detail in chap. 3.)

The Importance of Adequate Ventilation

One of the things that should be a feature of every child's bedroom is a good source of fresh air. A stuffy, overheated room is unhealthy and not conducive to restful sleep. If it is not possible to have an open window in your child's room, at least make sure that fresh air from the outside can get in by some other means. Opening the window in a nearby bathroom is just one solution to getting adequate ventilation.

It is also a good idea to have metal mesh screens installed on all windows. The brilliant invention of window screens is largely responsible for the eradication of malaria in the United States. Mosquitoes, however, still proliferate in many communities. Whether they carry malaria or not, mosquitoes are a dreadful nuisance and a potent cause of many a sleepless summer night. Not only will screens keep your house and your child's sleeping environment free of mosquitoes, they will keep most insects— whether bloodsucking or merely annoying—at bay without compromising the circulation of fresh air.

Fresh air is especially important if your house is heated by any form of fuel-burning device, such as a forced-air furnace, gas-burning stove, wood-burning stove, or fireplace. All devices that generate heat by combustion produce the deadly, odorless, and tasteless gas carbon monoxide. Be sure to have your furnace and fireplace checked regularly for carbon monoxide emissions. See that your furnace is kept spotlessly clean and change its filters frequently. Combustion devices that are out of regulation or dirty may produce deadly amounts of carbon monoxide without your ever suspecting it. If harsh weather conditions require that you use such heating devices at night, an open window allowing the free circulation of fresh air could be the difference between safety and tragedy.

When the air is hot and dry inside but cold and wet outside, you can expect your child to develop a stuffy nose. A cold can keep your child from sleeping, because children usually are not very good at breathing through their mouths. Also, the discomfort and inconvenience of a stuffy nose may interfere with sleep all on its own. Did you know that an artificially heated room may lose up to a gallon of water from the air every twenty-four hours? The lungs function best when the air you breathe is moist. If the air in the room itself is dry, the nose humidifies the air, but this process draws away precious bodily moisture from other parts of the body, leading to a state of physiological dehydration. It makes more sense to avoid this hazard by keeping the air in your child's room temperate and moist. For warmth in bed at night, use a better quality down comforter, more blankets, or have your child wear warmer and fleecier pajamas.

During the warmer months, sleeping with the windows open is equally important. The old-fashioned screened sleeping porches of older houses were a rational and healthful answer to the need for fresh air at night during good weather. If you are concerned that open windows might invite intruders, call your local police station and have an officer come to your home to give you tips on how to secure your home without compromising your need for fresh air. We all need to feel safe and secure when we fall asleep.

The Importance of Darkness

Another key element in making your child's room just right is darkness. Many parents will have read reports of the recent landmark study that found that children who sleep with illuminated night-lights or lamps in their rooms in their first two years are at greater risk of being nearsighted a few years later.[2] Our eyes seem to require the rest naturally imposed on them by the daily cycle of darkness. There are other, equally important reasons for maintaining darkness at night, which I have discussed in chapter 3. Sometimes, though, children do have to get up in the middle of the night to urinate. Simply for the purposes of navigating through a darkened house, a small, dim night-light in the bathroom or hallway is acceptable, but the bedroom should be dark in order to maintain the natural diurnal rhythms and promote restful sleep.

It is also a good idea if your bedroom door always remains unlocked and open for your child in case he needs you during the night. Always let your child know by thought, word, and deed that you will respond to him even if it is dark in the house.

When children are afraid of the dark, it is usually not the dark per se that they fear. It is that they have learned to associate the dark with feelings of abandonment, danger, and insecurity. It is best, of course, to spare your child from making this association in the first place by sleeping with your baby and cultivating an atmosphere of safety and security. Still, if a fear of the dark arises in childhood, this should be a clue that your child does not feel safe and secure. You should make a compassionate effort to uncover the causes of your child's fear. Then you can give your child the comfort she needs and allay her fears.

The Right Bed

We all know the importance of a good mattress. A child's bed should have the firmest mattress that you can buy. Studies have consistently shown an association between soft mattresses and sudden infant death syndrome (SIDS), also known as "cot death" or "crib death."[3–5] Infants who have unexpectedly died while sleeping on a soft mattress were probably unable to turn their heads to one side to maintain ventilation, due to the constriction of a soft mattress. Some studies have found a correlation between SIDS and sleeping on an old mattress, that is, one that has been previously used and discarded by another child or adult.[6] Sleeping on an old mattress may be an important factor, but it still needs confirmation before official recommendations can be made. Still, why take a chance? Until an association is either proved or disproved, you can do no wrong by playing it safe and providing your child with a new mattress of the highest quality. In short, whether your infant sleeps alone in his own bed or with you in yours, make sure that the mattress is new, firm, and in tip-top condition.

Waterbeds, especially older models, can be dangerous for infants and small children.[7,8] Infants have died while sleeping in waterbeds as a result of airway obstruction. Others have died by getting wedged between the water mattress and the waterbed frame or wall.[9] So, if your child is to sleep with you, in the interest of safety, replace your waterbed with a good, firm mattress. Even if your child sleeps alone, her bed should not be a waterbed. A waterbed is simply an unacceptable and inappropriate choice.

If your family sleeps on the floor on futons—Japanese style—you and your child will still benefit by spending a little more money getting the firmest and finest, 100 percent-cotton futon you can buy.

Parents and other adults should also refrain from sleeping on sofas with infants. This is especially true for adults who are either obese or drunk. In the medical literature, there are numerous reports of babies who have been found dead, wedged between a deeply unconscious adult (usually an obese or drunk adult) and the back cushions of a sofa.[10] This admonition is just a matter of common sense, but it is helpful to remind ourselves of it. Your baby's safety and sense of well-being depend on your using good sense at all times.

I think that it is also important that your child's bed sheets should be made of 100 percent natural fibers. So many of the flashy, theme-oriented sheets aimed at the children's market are either entirely or partially made of artificial fibers that do not allow your child's skin to breathe. They trap moisture and perspiration, ensuring that your child is hot and sweaty during the night. These conditions are unfavorable for good sleep. With 100 percent cotton sheets, warm air can circulate, keeping your child comfortable, safe, and dry.

Sheets should be changed at least once a week, and more often if they show the least sign of soiling. Stains of any kind act like a magnet to insects, most of which are too small for the eye to see, but large enough to cause irritation to skin, eyes, and lungs.

On the same note, beds should be made every morning to keep the sheets clean and free of debris, insects, dirt, and dust. A clean bed with clean sheets is a comfortable and safe bed.

The Right Sleepwear

Ideally, your child should sleep in a pair of 100 percent cotton pajamas or nightshirt, or in the nude. Your child's personal preferences, your family tradition, or weather conditions will determine what is most appropriate at any given time of year. The most important thing is that sleepwear should be clean, comfortable, and nonrestricting, yet not so billowy that a child could get tangled up and risk suffocation. Because infants do not yet have the muscle power or coordination to free themselves from clothing constrictions, form-fitting sleepers or nudity (with diaper if necessary) would seem to be among the right choices.

This is not the place to address in detail the tremendous controversy over the question of fire safety and children's sleepwear, but a few words are in order. Out of fear of fire, some parents have been encouraged to put their children in sleepwear that is advertised as being flame retardant. In fact, the government requires that newly manufactured garments designated and sold as children's sleepwear should be both flame retardant and self-extinguishing. The government, however, does not compel parents to dress their children in these sorts of garments. Most flame-retardant sleep garments are made of polyester that has been treated with flame-retardant chemicals, such as Tris (tris [2,3dibromopropyl] phosphate or tris [2-chloroethyl] phosphate). Unfortunately, this chemical is carcinogenic.[11,12] It can be absorbed through the skin or through the mouth if a child sucks or chews on a piece of a fabric treated with this chemical. There are also tremendous disadvantages to artificial fibers, which are uncomfortable and hot. Against the skin, they cause the body to sweat but do not allow the sweat to evaporate. These conditions will only aggravate your child, promote unhealthiness, and make sleep difficult.

We all acknowledge that it is far better for your child's health to be clad in 100 percent, chemical-free natural fibers, such as cotton or linen, but parents will have to weigh the risks and do what they think is best in their particular situation. Still, putting your child in chemically treated, 100 percent artificial fibers is no substitute for taking all the common-sense precautions you can to make your house fire safe. Nighttime house fires are almost always caused by preventable accidents, such as carelessly dropped cigarettes, unattended candles, accumulated garbage, overburdened electrical outlets, or portable electric heaters that have been left illuminated at night. None of these things is inevitable. Each is the result of negligence on the part of parents and can and should be prevented.

As a parent, it is your responsibility to do everything you can to reduce the risk of fire in your house, and this includes installing a smoke detector in your child's room, conducting regular fire drills, and outlining the evacuation plans for your child in the event of a fire. I think that it is better to use a little common sense and prevent fires in the first place than to argue over what sort of sleep garments burn slower. Telephone your local fire department to get the latest tips on making your house as safe from fire as possible.

The Right Sleeping Position

While we sleep, our basic bodily functions continue. Although our breathing takes on a different rhythm when we sleep, our need to breathe is just as vital. Certain sleeping positions promote good breathing, while others can hinder breathing. As they reach maturity, children will find their preferred sleeping position, or at least their preferred position for falling asleep, but for infants, only one sleeping position seems to be entirely safe.

Infants should sleep on their backs in the so-called "supine position." Sleeping on the abdomen ("prone sleeping") is associated with SIDS. In fact, the dramatic reduction in the rate of SIDS in recent years is attributed to the worldwide medical campaign to educate parents about the dangers of prone sleeping.[13]

The problem with prone sleeping seems to be that it can lead to difficulties with breathing. A baby can smother himself under his own weight, especially if sleeping on a soft mattress or a waterbed, or on any nonfirm surface. One of the many great benefits of sleeping with your baby is that it allows you to monitor the infant's sleeping position. A mother who finds that her baby unconsciously turns onto his abdomen during the night can gently return her baby to the supine position. Sleeping on the back is also better for the child's posture, as it encourages a straight back with correct curves for a strong healthy body. Also, sleeping on the back enables the small infant to awaken and still be able to look around at the environment. If an infant awakens on his abdomen, he will rub his head into the sheet with every movement. Many a rash on a baby's cheeks is resolved simply by changing to the supine position, especially when the infant is drooling and the sheet under his head becomes wet.

In summary, help your child get a good night's sleep by making your child's sleeping environment a sanctuary from the distractions of life and a bastion of comfort and safety. Our internal environment is a reflection of our external environment, and vice versa. Foster the feelings of security and confidence that will help your child sleep by making his bedroom clean, neat, peaceful, and safe from all perils and dangers.

Chapter 5

Things to Do During the Day to Foster a Good Night's Sleep

*A*good night's sleep is the culmination of a good day's activities. We have all noticed in ourselves that various joys and stresses encountered every day will affect how we sleep. If our day was filled with harmony, happiness, activity, proper nourishment, and fun, we can be assured of a good night's sleep. On the other hand, if we were inactive, undernourished (though not necessarily underfed), angry, distressed, restless, or depressed, we know that our sleep is unlikely to be restful. It is the same for your child. What your child has or has not done during the day will affect how he sleeps.

As a parent and a partner to your child, you are in the privileged position of being able to bring a measure of stability to your child's day. Your child is depending on you to make her day as harmonious and fulfilling as possible. You have the power to do this. Everything that you do to make your child's day as beautiful, wholesome, and invigorating as possible will be reflected in your child's sleep.

Our day's activities affect sleep not only on a psychological level but also on a neurological level. Our internal clock is set by our day's activities.

The hour at which we arise, the amount of sunlight to which we are exposed, the amount of exercise we have received, our diet, and many other factors reset our internal clock every day. If our internal clock has been set correctly, then, all other things being equal, we can be assured of a good night's sleep. This is just as true of adults as it is of children. As the guardians, nurturers, protectors, and guides of their children, parents have the responsibility of ensuring that their children's internal clock is correctly reset each day. Thankfully, this task is very easy to accomplish.

The Importance of Exercise

One simple, beneficial, and essential way to ensure a good night's sleep is to see that your child gets adequate exercise every day, preferably in the morning or afternoon. Right from the first day of your baby's life, you can exercise with your baby. Move his legs and arms in a gentle stretching manner. You might even try doing this to music or singing to your baby as he learns the things his body can do. You can stand him up on his legs without fearing that this will cause "bowed legs." You can gently bounce your baby on your lap and watch him smile as he enjoys the movement. Of course, exercising a baby should be done with great care. Never exercise your baby in a rough, violent, or jerking motion. Babies are extremely delicate, and we would not want to hurt them. If your baby cries, then stop your exercise workout immediately. If in doubt about any exercise, please consult a physical therapist or your pediatrician.

At my pediatric office in Los Angeles, we offer parents a weekly baby exercise class taught by a physical therapist from Children's Hospital of Los Angeles. Parents learn about the physical development of their baby, watch other parents exercise with their children, and learn how special their own baby is. Parents and babies really enjoy moving and exercising together. We also encourage parents to bathe with their baby, holding the baby in the tub as she splashes about. This is especially good for fathers who want to be more involved in the care of their children. Of course, infants and small children should never be left alone in a tub of water, nor should the water be too hot or too cold. Water temperature is very important for your baby. Just like Goldilocks's favorite bowl of porridge, it needs to be "just right."

One is never too young or too old for healthy exercise, and the best form of exercise is walking. Walking is the most natural and practical form of exercise for all of us. Take your child for a good walk every day. Even before your child can walk on his own, you should take him for a walk, holding him in your arms or wrapping him up against your body in a baby carrier, papoose, or sling. As long as your baby moves as you move, he will enjoy the contact, even if he falls asleep. You can take your baby wherever you go if he is strapped to you in this traditional manner.

Parents know from their own experience that being cooped up in the house all day is a guaranteed way of having restless sleep. Our human body requires exercise, not just to keep our muscles in tone and to keep our internal organs functioning properly, but to keep our brains working properly. Sleep, it must be remembered, is a function of the brain. It is for the brain's benefit that we go to sleep each night. Certainly, people who exert themselves physically all day, especially those who perform difficult labor, such as farmers, will need physical rest in addition to mental rest, but most of us today do not engage in physical labor. We spend most of our day sitting. For this reason, a daily regime of exercise is paramount for good health and good sleep.

There is now a spiritual movement in China called Qigong. An intricate part of Qigong is walking to cure disease, and, of course, great results are claimed by its practitioners. Still, it is interesting that Western science has discovered that, like sunshine, a morning walk triggers the production of the brain hormone melatonin,[1] which, as we have seen, is vital for regulating our daily sleep/wakefulness cycle.

Playing competitive games like tennis, football, soccer, baseball, or basketball may provide exercise and may be helpful in regulating the cycle of melatonin release,[2] but in the long term, the one who really wins is not the one who scored the most points but the one who got the most exercise. Many of these sports involve a lot of standing around and waiting, rather than real, sustained exercise. Competitive sports can also have the unpleasant effect of arousing negative emotions and unhealthy, aggressive, and adversarial attitudes toward others. Noncompetitive activities, such as walking, swimming, running, dancing, hiking, or gymnastics, all have the benefit of providing the entire body with a sustained workout without any of the unpleasant drawbacks associated with competitive sports. Whatever sporting activity your child enjoys, encourage her to use her muscles, not with the intention of triumphing over others, but with the aim of strengthening her own body and brain.

It is important, though, that both you and your children try to avoid strenuous exercise at night, because increased physical activity during the habitual rest period can disrupt circadian clock function. Irrespective of intensity, exercise near the offset of the normal nighttime cycle of melatonin secretion, i.e., during the morning and afternoon, has no consistent acute effect on the cycle or timing of melatonin secretion. It only beneficially increases the secretion of melatonin at night. Nighttime exercise, whether of moderate or high intensity, results in phase delays of the melatonin onset on the next evening, which may result in sleep disturbances.[3–5]

The most obvious benefit of walking is that it involves all the skeletal muscles as well as the cardiovascular system. Walking also gives the tendons that tether our muscles to the skeleton a beneficial stretch. We sometimes forget that walking is not just an exercise for our legs. We automatically swing our arms when we walk as well. This arm movement is not only good for our arms, but it appears that it is good for the brain. The rhythmic, alternating swinging of the arms sets up a neurological rhythm that stimulates both hemispheres of the brain, thereby fostering good neurological health.

For those of you who live in the countryside, walking may be a welcome necessity of life. Having your child accompany you while you walk from home to the village store and back, or as you walk along country lanes from one chore to the next, is a lovely way of seeing that your child gets sufficient exercise. It is also a great way to both socialize your child to the patterns of adult life and to invite your child's participation in your daily activities. Instead of simply having your child observe you watering the garden, water the garden together. Patiently and gently enfold your child into your life's activities. The added benefit of encouraging his active participation is that you and your child will get the exercise necessary to ensure a good night's sleep.

For those who live in the city, walking is equally a necessity of life. Walking trips from store to store, from office to office, or from school to home, are all part of the pattern of city life. Taking your child with you familiarizes him with his environment, teaches him survival skills that we all need in order to navigate our way through life, and stimulates his mind, as well as exercising his body. Doing things together with your child builds up the store of shared experiences that are vital for good relationships.

Being a parent does not merely mean producing a child from the fusion of genetic material from mother and father. It does not merely mean meeting the immediate survival needs of your child. Being a parent requires that we invest deeply in the relationship between parent and child. Good parents show children how to be a good person, a good citizen, and a good neighbor. Sharing activities means sharing lives and transmitting the parents' store of wisdom and experience. The physical aspect of these daily activities will not only enrich the relationship between parent and child, it will make sleep better and more rewarding. In those families where the parents, for one reason or another, spend very little time with their children, I suspect that some of the resistance children put up to going to bed is simply a tactic they have evolved to prolong their contact with their parents. Sometimes, children would rather have unhappy and conflict-filled contact with their parents than have no contact at all. Having your child walk with you and participate in your daily errands will do much to meet your child's need to spend time with you.

When you take your child with you on your errands, make her an active participant. Tell your child, for example, that you need her help to choose the right kind of carrots for dinner. Ask your child to pick the ripest melon, the nicest-looking loaf of bread. If you are going to the bank, bring your child into your confidence. Tell her that you are depositing or withdrawing a certain amount of money so that you can pay the rent, or the groceries, or the electricity bill.

It really does not matter what the errand is. Children want and need to participate in the intimate details of family life. Some parents treat their children as guests in their own home. They cater to the child's physical needs but do not bring the child into the deeper levels of family involvement. Involving your child in the business of running a family or a household will not only strengthen the familial bond, it will require your child to accompany you on your errands. This translates into beneficial exercise and a more varied array of stimuli for the brain. Consequently, it will result in a better night's sleep for your child.

For those parents who live in suburbs, getting adequate exercise, ironically, is often much more difficult. The suburban plan of living was largely created, almost overnight, in the post–World War II building boom. It is a plan of living entirely dependent on the automobile, since the vast housing estates that have become such a conspicuous part of American life are not self-sufficient social and economic units. Suburban neighborhoods, by design, are devoid of shops and businesses where residents can perform their daily errands. Taking a walk through a suburban development becomes an end unto itself. It has no utilitarian function. Consequently, few suburbanites walk enough. Families have little choice but to climb into the car and drive long distances to shop. Children have to be driven to school and driven to friends' houses. The devastation that this way of life has had on physical health can be measured by the alarming rise in the number of clinically obese suburban children and by the rise, or the perceived rise, in sleep problems. Without adequate physical exercise, adequate restful sleep is most unlikely.

The number of suburban American children these days who could not walk a mile if their lives depended on it is distressing, in large measure, because their lives do, in fact, depend on it. We have all heard the old stories of children who had to walk (usually barefoot, or so the stories go) several miles to school each morning and yet thought nothing of it. Despite the mythic dimension of these stories, they contain an important element: namely, that children have the physical capability of walking great distances. When in a state of health, they have terrific stamina and endurance. All things being equal, walking such distances sets children up for a lifetime of good cardiovascular health. It also meets the requirements for physical activity that ensure a good night's sleep.

What can suburban parents do? Parents with babies and toddlers can establish good exercise patterns by taking their children on a nice long walk around the block every day. Make the walk educational. You can explore nature. Hunt for different kinds of trees, flowers, plants, or leaves. You might look for birds. Vary the focus and route of the walks, but make them interesting to your child. If your child likes plants, have a knowledgeable friend walk with you and your child to help you identify the flowers and trees in your neighbors' gardens. Alternatively, get a good garden book with pictures so that you and your child together can try to identify the different species of flowers and trees. Such activities will strengthen the bond between parent and child and, important for our purposes here, meet the need for physical activity, which is so important for sleep.

Additionally, encourage your children to play outdoors as much as possible. Children are naturally very active when outside. Leave them to their own devices, and they will run, jump, climb, and explore. Provide your child with every opportunity to enjoy outdoor life. Install a swing set and activity center in your backyard. Families in the warmer parts of the country may have their own swimming pool or have access to a public swimming pool nearby. Like walking, swimming is a healthy and fun way to get exercise. Have your child invite lots of friends over to play in order to maximize the level of activity. I can assure you that the greater the level of physical activity in your child's day, the better and more restful will be your child's sleep.

For families who live where rough winters make playing outdoors difficult, there are a wide variety of activities that children can engage in at home that will meet their need for exercise. Old-fashioned calisthenics, such as jumping jacks or running in place, are simple and appropriate ways for your child to get the necessary dose of physical activity. Make it fun by turning it into a family activity. You can follow the exercises on a commercially available exercise videotape. Many tapes are made especially for children. Fancy and expensive exercise equipment is unnecessary, but you might consider investing in a simple exercise bicycle.

Boys and girls both love to roughhouse, though it is my experience that boys seem to initiate it more often than girls. Roughhousing and friendly wrestling are a terrific way for both parent and child to get some exercise in the house. It also necessitates physical contact between parent and child, and physical contact is extremely important for your child's mental health.

Physical activities, as I mentioned above, should be encouraged in the morning and early afternoon rather than at dinnertime or bedtime. Getting your children excited and physically exhausted before bedtime will make it difficult for them to calm down enough to fall asleep easily, no matter how tired they may be.

As part of waking up from a good night's sleep, you might try taking a family walk in the park, garden, or just around the block, before breakfast, and before everyone goes off to daily activities. A morning walk is a good idea even if you need to get out of bed just a little earlier to do it.

The Importance of Sunshine

Exposure to sunshine in the morning regulates the normal production cycle of the beneficial brain chemical melatonin in the evening, establishing the normal diurnal cycle, called the circadian rhythm.[6–8] In addition to the indole hormone melatonin, sunshine also influences the production of other important brain chemicals, such as the indole neurotransmitter serotonin and the peptide neurohormone corticotropin releasing hormone (CRH), which also play important roles in maintaining the sleep/wakefulness cycle.[9] Production of vitamin D_3, the hormone of sunlight, is also important for mental health, adequate sleep, and the prevention of insomnia. Exposure to sunlight leads to the production of vitamin D_3, which, in turn, leads to beneficial changes in serotonin levels.[10] If you are able to take your child on a morning walk, your child will, no doubt, be exposed to enough sunlight to ensure a restful night's sleep. Even on cloudy days, ultraviolet light from the sun beams down to earth unimpeded, so make sure some of it falls on your child.

Although dermatologists have warned us of the danger of getting too much sun, most of us, in fact, are in danger of getting too little sun. Many of us are getting less sunshine in our lives every year as we spend our days going from house to car to office, barely stepping out into the sunlight at all. Naturally, we should avoid getting a sunburn, and, additionally, we should try to avoid staying out in the summer sun between 10 A.M. and 2 P.M.—the period during which the ultraviolet rays of the sun are strongest—but most of us, including our children, would benefit from a little more sunlight in our daily lives. My mother used to tell me to get lots of sunshine so that I would develop properly. She knew nothing about vitamin D_3 or melatonin, but she instinctively had the right idea about the importance of sunlight on human growth.

Studies have also shown that sunshine entering the eye and falling on the bare skin has the beneficial effect of maintaining and restoring the proper balance of brain chemicals that are responsible for optimum mental health.[11-13] Patients who suffer from clinical depression have enjoyed remarkable improvement just by increasing their daily exposure to sunlight. I think we can all agree that if sunshine can cure, it can also prevent some mental health problems, such as depression.

I am not sure that boredom can be classified as a mental health problem, but we all know how debilitating boredom can be, and we have all seen how miserable bored children are. Just think back to those times when you yourself were painfully bored when cooped up in the house all day and denied the feel of sunshine on your face. Do you remember how poorly you slept as a consequence? Your child will suffer in the same way, only I suspect that any child will complain louder. For your own mental health, you will find that getting your child outside as much as possible for some fresh air, sunshine, and exercise will be beneficial. It will also, necessarily, translate into a good night's sleep.

The Importance of Proper Nutrition

A nutritious diet is necessary at all times and for every reason imaginable, but it is especially important for healthful sleep. You know from personal experience how poorly you sleep after an unhealthful or insufficient meal. You know all too well that just because you are eating does not mean that you are getting nourishment. Like sleeping, eating is one of the basic requirements of life. The wonderful thing about the requirements for life—and I refer to the requirements for sustaining our own life and for sustaining the life of the human species—is that they are pleasurable. This is nature's clever way of encouraging us to engage in these necessary activities. If eating were not as pleasurable as it is, we would neglect our need to eat, and then we would die.

It is a safe rule that any food that tastes good in its raw and natural state, as it is produced in nature, is nutritious. Think of how delicious a ripe peach is as you hold it in your mouth and savor its nectar. Think of the delicious nutty creaminess of a perfectly ripe Haas avocado. Just imagine yourself drinking the sweet juice of a freshly squeezed orange. The pleasure you experience is nature's way of enticing you into consuming the very things that are the most nutritious and vital for your health.

Your taste buds protect you from the many natural poisons in the environment by giving them a taste that your brain automatically interprets as bitter. Unripe fruit is painfully sour. The smell and taste of rotten food stimulate receptors in your nose and mouth that signal your brain that you are in danger of consuming molds and bacteria harmful to health. This is why rotten food smells and tastes so horrible, causing you automatically to spit it out.

If we lived in a natural state in a bounteous natural environment, we would have little trouble guaranteeing that all the food we ate was nutritious. Nowadays, getting adequate nutrition takes a little more effort. Many of the most unnourishing and harmful "foods" are designed by their manufacturers to mimic the nutrient triggers of natural foods. Fast-food hamburgers, for instance, have been shrewdly designed to have just the right combination of sweetness, saltiness, and creaminess to stimulate the appetite and make us think that we are eating something that is good for us. Soft drinks are designed to trick the brain and taste receptors into accepting the product as if it were a natural fruit juice, which is something that the body is automatically designed to crave and enjoy. If the artificial chemicals in soft drinks were not masked by powerful flavor and sweetening agents, their taste would be so horrible that no one could endure it. Some French fries have become favorites with children because they have been dipped in a sugar solution before they are deep-fried in processed grease. It is unfortunate that some Americans believe they are purchasing a meal at a fast-food establishment when they buy a double bacon cheeseburger, French fries, and a milk shake. In reality, they are taking the first steps toward coronary bypass surgery. A diet that is more than 30 percent fat has no place in a child's world. If you want to raise a healthy child, feed your child proper food.

Most of these factory-made products are aimed at children. The advertising campaigns that fuel sales and stimulate demand for these products are also aimed at children. Consequently, it can be difficult for parents to convince their children that they are protecting them when they refuse to buy these products. As difficult as it is for parents to resist the pleas of their children who have been lured by cunning advertising or by flashy packaging on store shelves, resist they must if they are serious about having healthy children who sleep well.

Of course, I realize that many people will protest, saying that they allow their kids to drink unlimited amounts of soft drinks and eat vast quantities of junk food, and yet their kids have never had a problem sleeping. I would reply that many children, like most humans, are equipped with a survival mechanism that enables them to endure almost any form of hardship and degradation, be it nutritional or otherwise. But just because we *can* endure hardship and degradation does not mean that we *should* or that there are no long-term consequences to having endured systematic malnutrition. The habitual consumption of artificial, factory-created, denatured, fractured, and unnatural pseudo-food can only lead to malnourishment and ill health, regardless of the amount of supplemental vitamins and minerals that may be added to the mix. The fact that manufacturers *have* to add vitamins and minerals to their products only proves that these items are inherently inferior and best not served to children. Why give your child a fatty, salty, sugary, artificially colored, artificially flavored, cholesterol-laden hamburger that has had powdered, factory-made, synthetic vitamins mixed into it, when you can give your child a nutritious, delicious, wholesome, juicy apple, for instance, that has loads of natural vitamins, minerals, and other vital elements as a constituent part of it? Stirring synthetic vitamins and minerals into lard does not make lard nutritious. Even if you stirred more vitamins and minerals into lard than are found in an apple, that still would not make it more nutritious than an apple.

It is simple to teach your children to distinguish between pseudo-food products and real food: Simply talk to your child. Instead of just banning non-nutritious junk products and soft drinks from your house, explain to your child why such things are unhealthy. Explain how lucky your child is to be smart enough to tell the difference between good food and junk products. I guarantee you that your child will take pride in his excellent diet and superior nutrition as long as you include him in the educational process. Explain in a calm voice how important nutrition is and why it is your pleasure as a parent to provide your child with good-tasting, nutritious, and delicious real food. Make every meal a treat and an exciting culinary excursion so that junk food will never seem like a treat, but like an unacceptable burden. Not only will your child benefit, but you will benefit too, because you will be providing your child with the nutritional foundation for good sleep. If your child sleeps well, so will you.

Good natural foods are loaded with lots of important vitamins and minerals. It is unhelpful to suggest that any particular nutrient is any more important than another. We need them all. Still, one nutrient that is important for sleep is magnesium, which has been called "Nature's muscle relaxant." In infants, studies have found a correlation between serum magnesium in the bloodstream and sleep phase.[14] Infants with greater concentrations of serum magnesium had increased periods of quiet sleep and decreased periods of active sleep. There were also corresponding correlations between serum magnesium and rapid eye movements, submental muscle tone, and gross body movements. This is important information for parents who want their infants to get good-quality sleep. Thankfully, adequate dietary magnesium is easy to get. The best sources of magnesium are green leafy vegetables, salad, and "green foods," such as the various algae and seaweed products now available. A "green" drink or a fresh green salad for mother in the evening when she is breast-feeding will help impart to nursing babies the magnesium and other nutrients they need for healthful sleep. Weaned and weaning children also benefit from a diet rich in salads and other green things.

Another essential trace element is selenium. Like magnesium, selenium is necessary for proper brain function, immune response, and, of course, sleep. Foods naturally rich in selenium are root vegetables such as carrots. Celery is also a good source of selenium. The richest source of selenium, however, is Brazil nuts. Thankfully, these tasty nuts can be conveniently purchased with their heavy shells already removed. When your child is old enough to properly chew nuts and swallow them without choking, add a few raw, unsalted Brazil nuts to your child's meals or snacks. This will have multiple benefits, including a good night's sleep.

A Sense of Purpose and Inclusion

While the body's need for proper nutrition and exercise is always present, the underlying psychological need for safety and security is deeply associated with these physical needs. If bedtime rituals are intended to underscore the message that your child is loved, safe, and secure, the things you do with your child in the daytime should also be infused with this critically important message. Your baby, as a fetus in the mother's womb, was attached to the mother through the umbilical cord and the placenta. The baby and the mother were one unit. After birth, they still remain one unit. Birth is not a separation of the mother from her child, but an evolution in the organization of their union. The baby may now live outside the mother's body and may receive its nourishment from the breast rather than through the umbilical cord, but the union between mother and baby has not ended. Neither babies nor children can survive on their own. The baby is still entirely dependent on the mother for nourishment, warmth, safety, and security.

Gradually, at her own pace, a baby will wean herself from her complete dependence on her mother, slowly attaching to her father and establishing solid relationships with others. This is all a part of normal psychosocial development. Like birds, we are altricial animals, born dependent on our parents for nourishment, safety, and security. We are confined to the "nest" until we have completed our physical, psychological, emotional, and intellectual development.

We should not take the uncharitable view that children are unnecessarily needy or insecure. Instead, we should remind ourselves that children, like adults, share the same human needs for love, safety, and security. The more love, comfort, security, and safety you give your child, the stronger will be his personal fortitude, the greater his level of confidence, and the greater his self-esteem. When a baby learns to associate his dependence on his parents with dependability, he will have the confidence to venture forth and explore the world, never fearing that his parents will abandon him if he dares remove himself from their presence. When a baby takes those first adventurous crawls away from mother and toward an object of curiosity, he will turn and look back every few seconds to make sure mother is still there. Once he learns that mother will always be there, he will move farther away and look back less often.

So it is with sleep. The more your child has been encouraged to evolve a sense that she can always depend on her parents, the less likely she will be to associate bedtime and sleep with abandonment. Fostering that sense of dependability is the key to building your child's confidence and independence. This means holding your baby immediately after birth and never being separated from your baby. It means taking your baby with you wherever you go. In Asia, babies are traditionally held in a fabric sling around the parent's or grandparent's back. The child is in a constant state of physical contact with the parent. This exchange of touch, sensation, and bodily warmth is the key to building dependability. Parents in most traditional societies also sleep with their infants and children. In chapter 7, I will go into this issue in greater detail, but suffice it to say here that co-sleeping has the obvious advantage of allowing bodily contact to continue, without a break, every hour of the day and night.

Beyond the physical and psychological importance of maintaining physical contact with your child, there are powerful cultural benefits to be gained as well. Taking your child with you during your day's activities teaches your child what it is to be a human. It shows your child what people do during the day in your particular culture. The child's mind is designed to take in as much sensory information as possible. Holding your child against your body and taking him with you as you do your daily errands, chores, and activities is the greatest form of entertainment and education a baby can know. For the very young child, being held by the mother as she makes her way through the world gives the child the vital sensation of movement. The rhythm of walking, sitting, bending, or running is familiar to every baby because, after all, life in the womb was one of constant movement. Movement, then, is familiar, expected, and necessary. As you walk around with your baby slung on your back or strapped to your front, you will find that your baby is not in the least bothered by the constant motion and rocking. On the contrary, he is perfectly able to sleep or to observe the fascinating world that you take him through.

Similarly, including your older child in your daily activities gives her a sense of purpose and inclusion that will build and reinforce her sense of your dependability, the dependence of all family members on each other, and her personal independence. Bedtime, under these circumstances, will never seem like a deprivation because her day has been so psychologically and spiritually fulfilling. It is crucial to give your child 100 percent of your time. This does not mean that you must give up your own life. It means that you include your child in your life. As educator and author Jeannine Parvati Baker says, when you have a child, you are not getting a possession: You are getting a relationship. That relationship begins at conception and should continue in its intensity and beauty long after birth. The relationship, of course, will evolve and entail differing responsibilities, but if it is healthy, it will be mutually beneficial and enriching. The cornerstone of that relationship is dependability, which is fostered by including your child in your world, taking your baby with you wherever you go, and maintaining constant physical contact between parent and child. As your child grows and matures, her need for constant physical contact will diminish, but I can assure you that you will not regret a single moment spent with your child in such beautiful intimacy.

Helping your child to overcome or avoid sleep disturbances cannot, therefore, be considered an isolated problem, unrelated to the rest of life. Sleep is completely interrelated with every other element in your child's life. Good sleep is just as much about a good child/parent relationship as it is about good sleep hygiene. Clearly, many parents today simply do not have the opportunity to spend as much time with their children and infants as they would like, but your parent surrogates—be they grandparents, neighbors, baby-sitters, or day care attendants—can all be instructed and expected to do as much for your child's well-being as you would yourself. Naturally, it would be better if your baby could spend all his time with you, but if that is unachievable, it is essential that your baby spend his time with another active human being so that the vital process of acculturation can occur. Instruct your baby-sitter to strap your baby to her back and move around, walk, and go on errands, just as you would if you were free to do so. No baby should be left alone in a crib or playpen, unattended, untouched, or unstimulated. Every moment spent moving through the world with an active adult is filled with revelation for a baby. If your baby is getting his daily requirement of stimulation, activity, movement, physical contact, and observation, he will be better prepared to sleep restfully at night, for he will have suffered none of the frustrations brought on by boredom and sensory deprivation. He will sleep soundly and securely, according to the sleep pattern appropriate to his age and stage of physical development, because he intuitively recognizes that his innate human biological expectations are being met. For older children, the same needs exist, though in altered form, depending on the child's current state of psychological development. From birth on, make your child a valuable, valued, and intimate partner in your life and I assure you that your child will be as free from the specter of sleep disturbances as anyone could ever hope to be.

Chapter 6

Positive Bedtime Rituals for a Good Night's Sleep

*B*edtime can be one of the most enjoyable parts of your child's day. One of the best ways to make bedtime a special time that your child will anticipate with pleasure is to incorporate gentle, peaceful, and calming rituals or ceremonies into your child's evening routine. Effective rituals calm the mind and relax the body. They strengthen the bond between parent and child and thereby strengthen the family unit. Bedtime rituals reinforce the essential feelings of safety and security. Every child, every adult, even every animal needs to feel safe and secure to enjoy a peaceful sleep. This is one of the preconditions for happiness, good health, and relaxation.

If positive bedtime rituals are not observed in the family, the child may have the misfortune of associating bedtime with separation from parents and loved ones. Bedtime may seem like a punishment. Children may feel that, by being sent to bed, they are "missing out on all the fun." Bedtime should be all the fun, and pleasant bedtime rituals can make this possible.

Even if your child does not have any problems falling asleep or staying asleep throughout the night, bedtime rituals are always a welcome addition. They may not necessarily help children sleep better, but they can definitely make children and parents happier by reducing the possibility that a child will resist going to sleep in the first place.

Although the following rituals are primarily intended to make bedtime a pleasant, positive, and beautiful experience for your child, they are also very effective for helping a child with genuine, clinically diagnosed sleep problems to overcome them. Sleep, as we have seen, is, in many respects, a matter of habit and pattern. Establishing positive new patterns will free your child from old negative patterns. It is true that many so-called sleep problems are usually caused by the parents holding unrealistic expectations—such as that children should naturally and without interaction from parents be willing to go to bed at a preordained time every evening, fall asleep immediately, and sleep the entire night through without interruption. I do not know the origin of these unrealistic expectations, but some parents simply have not been informed of the importance of establishing positive bedtime rituals in their child's life.

The issue of bedtime struggles, or a child resisting going to bed, has become recognized as the second most important "sleep problem" these days (the first most important "problem" being night waking). A child who absolutely refuses to go to bed and fall asleep or who awakens every two hours certainly is creating problems but is not necessarily suffering from a medical condition, as the term *sleep problem* implies.

One of the very nicest things about bedtime rituals is that they permit parents or other loved ones to spend quality time with their children. You should introduce these rituals in infancy, even before your baby can understand your words. Even without language, your infant knows how to communicate nonverbally. The bond of communication that you establish with your infant will expand and become richer as your child grows and develops language skills. All the effort that you put forth in these early weeks and months will be returned to you in the form of a deeply meaningful, rewarding, and long-lasting bond of love between you and your child.

I would not want anyone to mistake these lovely rituals for "tools" designed to trick children into "behaving." They are methods for bringing parents and children together. They allow children to enjoy the company of their parents, and they allow parents the privilege of getting to know and appreciate their children for the miracle that they are.

Some parents may fear that establishing these positive bedtime rituals will only make it impossible for their children to fall asleep on those occasions when parents or loved ones are unavailable or when circumstances are altered. This may include instances when the parents leave the child with a baby-sitter, or when the family has guests and the parents feel that it would be inhospitable to leave the guests alone while they attend to their children, or when the child is an overnight guest in someone else's house. These are not insurmountable obstacles.

Baby-sitters can easily be instructed to perform the child's favorite bedtime rituals. Choose a baby-sitter who knows how to tell stories, run baths, rub backs, or sing lullabies. Children will relish the opportunity to strengthen the bond of love and friendship with a favorite baby-sitter by means of these rituals. Children enjoy variety, and they have an almost infinite capacity for feeling and expressing love for a wide variety of people outside the immediate nuclear family.

In the other scenario—where parents feel that they have obligations to guests that must take precedence over their obligation to their children—there are a wide variety of solutions. You need not have any hesitation in excusing yourself from a guest for the amount of time it takes to lull your child to sleep. My friend Helen, the mother of five beautiful children, regularly has guests over for dinner. When her children were little, after the evening meal, Helen would politely excuse herself so that she could spend time with her children, talking to them quietly and telling them stories as they drifted off to sleep, while her husband entertained the guests by himself. On the rare occasion that a guest remarked on the amount of time that she had been gone, she would calmly explain that one of the joys of being a parent was getting to spend quality time with her children at bedtime. Her guests were always charmed by her lovely attitude. None was ever made to feel inhospitably treated. On the contrary, all were made to feel more welcome by being included into the warmth of Helen's family life.

If your child is invited to sleep somewhere other than his own bed at home, he will adapt. Children are very adaptable, and they usually love spending the night at their friends' houses.

Establishing a Reasonable Bedtime

Given that children require at least ten hours of sleep each night, set your child's bedtime at an appropriate hour so that she gets all the sleep she needs. If, for instance, your child must arise at 7:00 in the morning to get ready for school, and if your child needs only ten hours of sleep, then she will need to be asleep by 9:00 in the evening. This means, however, that you will need to start your bedtime rituals an hour or more before this time. A "bedtime" of 8:00, then, will enable you to spend a lovely hour of bedtime rituals with your child before she actually falls asleep at 9:00.

Your child may need more than ten hours of sleep. Long before your child is old enough to begin school, you will generally have ascertained how many hours of sleep he usually needs each night to awaken refreshed and remain alert during the day without becoming drowsy or cranky. There is also little harm in erring on the side of caution and allowing for a longer sleep time than your child actually needs. A healthy child will wake up when his sleep debt has been paid off. If he should wake up earlier than his appointed rising time, you can suggest that he use the time profitably and comfortably reading quietly in bed. For younger children, you may find it more convenient simply to readjust their bedtime. Older children can be taught to make their beds, bathe, dress, and feed themselves in the morning with the quietness, lightness, and respect due to those who may still be sleeping.

As in so many other areas of child raising, let your child know what your expectations are, gently and patiently show him how to meet these expectations, and then have the good sense to trust him to meet them on his own. Avoid the mistake of getting angry and punishing your child for getting up too early or failing to make the bed as neatly as a hotel maid would do it. Show him how to make the bed with the same amount of patience and good cheer that you would have appreciated when you were the same age. Have the good grace to recognize that we all make mistakes and that no one is perfect. The efficiency and skill with which your children carry out tasks such as making the bed will be directly related to your attitude in teaching and monitoring these tasks. A child is more likely to try hardest to please you if you are pleasant and liberal with praise and positive encouragement.

A Warm Bath Before Bed

A nice warm bath or shower before bedtime is a delightful, relaxing, and healthful way of inducing sleep for children as well as adults. Children tend to get quite dirty during the day, and it is important to cleanse the body thoroughly before climbing into bed. Going to bed with unclean skin and hair is not only unhealthy and unsanitary, it is irritating and, therefore, liable to hinder sleep. Still, whether your child is dirty or not, an evening bath has many additional benefits.

A nightly bath soothes the body, cleanses the skin, invigorates the respiratory system, and relaxes the mind. To make the bath even more relaxing, try adding a few drops of lavender oil to the water. The rich aroma is said to induce deep, restful sleep. Adding a little baking soda (sodium bicarbonate) to the water may soothe some irritated skin conditions. Traditionally, some Chinese parents add just a little ginger to the bathwater when the child has a mild upper respiratory infection or cold.

I always advise parents to avoid giving their children bubble baths. Bubble baths may have glamorous associations, thanks to Hollywood movies, and they are heavily marketed to children through television advertising, but they irritate and dry out the skin. Irritated skin means a poor night's sleep. Bubble baths can even cause urinary tract infections.[1] I suspect that many cases of bladder irritation and inflammation, as well as urinary tract irritation, are often misdiagnosed and treated as bacterial infections, when, in fact, they are just the symptoms of irritation caused by bubble baths and harsh soap. These would be more easily and more appropriately treated by simply stopping the bubble baths rather than mis-using antibiotics. I might add, for those American parents who have heard otherwise, that male circumcision does not prevent urinary tract infections in boys[2,3] nor does female circumcision prevent urinary tract infections in girls, as has been espoused by primitive and misguided teachings. The pre-vention of urinary tract infections depends on proper nutrition and proper hygiene, part of which means avoiding bubble baths and exposure to harsh chemicals in soap or overly chlorinated pool water. Bathe your child in pure, clean, fresh water.

Some families enjoy climbing into the bathtub together as an enjoy-able, playful, harmonious, and healthy family activity. You can also increase your child's enjoyment of the bath by adding toys, such as sailboats or other floating toys. Naturally, we would not want our children to play in the bathtub with battleships, military submarines, or war instruments of any kind at bedtime, as we want to encourage a peaceful, gentle, and relaxed frame of mind.

Although the benefits of soaking the entire body in warm water are obvious, showers are an equally valuable alternative. One benefit of a shower is that soapy wastewater is immediately washed down the drain, sparing your child from wallowing in dirty water. If your child is dirty but prefers a bath to a shower, do as the Japanese do: Get into an empty tub, rinse the body with warm water, soap up, scrub off the dirt, and rinse off completely. Then, fill the tub with warm water in which to soak.

The Importance of Special Bedtime Attire

Changing out of one's clothes and into special attire (or no attire) for bed is an effective ritual for focusing the mind and inducing sleep. It is prob-ably unimportant whether your child sleeps in a nightshirt, pajamas, or in the nude. Weather conditions will determine what form of attire, if any, is best at any given time of the year. It is important only that your child does not sleep in her clothes, especially the clothes she was wearing during the day. This includes underwear. If your child sleeps in underwear, make sure that it is a fresh pair rather than the pair she was wearing during the day. Sleeping in daytime clothes is not only unsanitary and unhealthy, it deprives a child of the psychological benefits to be gained by establishing a simple and clear demarcation between wakefulness and sleep.

Bedtime Stories

Reading or telling stories to your children while they are curled up in bed or snuggled in your lap is another important and effective way of inducing sleep. Reading has long-term benefits as well. Children whose parents read to them grow up to be adults who read. Interestingly, children who enjoy reading were read to as babies.[4] I imagine that most people would not think of reading to a baby, who, after all, does not seem to appreciate books or narratives. Actually, babies do appreciate stories. Even if they do not follow the narrative, they are keenly listening to the sound of your voice. They are learning the cadence and flow of the language. They are, in fact, absorbing vocabulary.

If parents speak a foreign language, it is important to read and speak to your baby in that language in addition to the language of the nation in which you live. The human brain, even the brain of a baby, is perfectly able to distinguish between one language and another. The wonderful benefit of reading or speaking to your baby in a foreign language is that your baby will learn to speak that language with little difficulty and will be entirely free of any accent. It is a regrettable fact that people who learn a foreign language after puberty almost never speak that language without an accent. Learning a foreign language in school after puberty is also very hard work. No reasonable person will deny the important advantages to be gained by speaking one or more foreign languages fluently.

Naturally, I do not have to tell you that scary tales or any story that might agitate your child are best avoided at bedtime. This does not, however, mean that fairy tales should be avoided. On the contrary, fairy tales should be the staple elements in your storytelling repertoire. Fairy tales, such as the tales recorded by the Brothers Grimm, are among our most ancient and valuable links to our distant past. Fairy tales contain deeply embedded symbols, myths, and images that reflect what it is to be human. Children unconsciously absorb and decode the rich language of symbols and signs in fairy tales. Even the less tranquil elements in some fairy tales, such as the menacing wolves, dens of thieves, wicked witches, and so forth, do not have the power to frighten children. Instead, these elements reveal to children, in a symbolic way, the ancient and enduring mysteries that have shaped human experiences. Tales such as "Little Red Riding Hood" express age-old awe about the mysteries of the forest. This tale also explains the importance of family relationships. Even on the surface level, fairy tales revolve around the resolution of problems and, as such, are richly satisfying to the child's mind. Children are immeasurably enriched when they are made familiar with this wonderful heritage.

Children also love having poetry read to them at bedtime. Likewise, the great classics of modern children's literature should form part of the staple repertoire of your child's bedtime rituals. Classics such as *Goodnight Moon* have appealed to younger children for generations. Older children may enjoy having their parents read them one or more chapters each night from a longer classic, such as *Charlotte's Web, Tom Sawyer, The Secret Garden, Heidi,* or *Charlie and the Chocolate Factory*. I know of one family that enjoys a nightly ritual of having the children gather around their father while he reads a chapter from *The Hobbit*. Because of the good, bond-strengthening habits set down by these parents, their children have always looked forward to going to bed each night.

All my children always looked forward to their bedtime, when they would hear another chapter of a favorite story, which was continued the following night until the book was finished. Sometimes, they would request to go to bed just so they could find out what would happen next in the story. Not only did this practice help them fall asleep easily, but it gave them an abiding interest in reading that has carried over to adulthood. When my children were older, they enjoyed my reading to them the works of Mark Twain and the Sherlock Holmes stories of Sir Arthur Conan Doyle. The enjoyment of having a parent or loved one read at bedtime does not diminish as the years go by. Even teenagers enjoy the entertainment value of a good story at bedtime, and although many teenagers may be loath to admit it, they also enjoy the lovely feeling of closeness between parent and child that is so strong during bedtime readings.

The Benefits of Music

A lullaby is a proven way of helping babies and children fall asleep. Parents have always sung their children to sleep. Even animals lull their offspring to sleep with special vocalizations. The deep purr of the mother cat has the effect of lulling her kittens to sleep.

Music is an emotion-based product of the mind. It affects the deepest structures in the human brain. The choice of music, therefore, is very important. Babies respond best to soothing, quiet melodies. If you play recorded music for your child, you will find that children prefer Mozart, Brahms, Debussy, or other soft and gentle classical melodies. If you play the piano, try playing relaxing pieces at bedtime. Soft classical music has the effect of focusing the attention of the mind and inducing a deep state of relaxation and calm. Bach composed his famous Goldberg Variations for this very purpose.

A recent series of studies have found that the music of Mozart is especially conducive to boosting brain power. According to an article in the journal *New Scientist*,[5] at the University of Illinois Medical Center, neurologist John Hughes and a musicologist colleague analyzed hundreds of compositions by Mozart, Chopin, and fifty-five other composers. Hughes predicted that sequences repeating regularly every twenty to thirty seconds may trigger the strongest response in the brain, because many functions of the central nervous system—such as the onset of sleep and brain wave patterns—also occur in thirty-second cycles. Hughes found that of all the music analyzed, Mozart most often peaks every thirty seconds. It is estimated that Mozart's music is encoded with this particular brain pattern because he started composing when he was only four years old, an age at which he might have best been able to tap into this inherent neural structure.

The old-fashioned lullaby, sung by the parent to the child, is still one of the nicest ways of lulling your child to sleep with music. Parents need not limit their repertoire to the standard lullabies, such as "Hush Little Baby, Don't Say a Word." A pleasing melody and a soft and gentle tone are the elements that matter most. Singing to your child opens up a deeply personal level of communication that is magical. It is as beautiful for the parent as it is for the child. One father told me that he could still remember the German lullaby that his mother sang to him every night as he fell asleep, even though he never did learn to speak German.

It is best not to think of children as animals that can or should be "trained" or "conditioned" to perform certain tricks, but as humans we do make associations between things. You can help your child associate that feeling of relaxation, calm, and safety necessary for sleep by singing or humming the same soothing lullaby each time your child wakes up in the middle of the night and needs to be lulled back to sleep or when your infant awakens to nurse. Sing softly to your baby while you nurse, and your baby will eventually learn to associate your song with the security and peace that make sleep desirable.

The Benefits of Massage and the Beauty of Physical Affection

Humans thrive on touch. Not surprisingly, it has been shown that if babies (especially preterm babies) are deprived of touch, they are more likely to fail to thrive—a dangerous syndrome that can lead to death without swift intervention.[6] The medical literature, in fact, is filled with studies documenting that the most beneficial form of touch is skin-to-skin contact between child and parent.[7–11] Research projects in Western Europe and the United States provide data demonstrating that infants held skin-to-skin have more regular heart rate and respirations, more deep sleep and alert inactivity, less crying, fewer infections, and greater weight gain. In addition, breast-feeding is more productive and of greater duration. Furthermore, fathers and mothers who maintain skin-to-skin contact with their babies become more quickly attached to their infants and feel more confident about caring for them.[12]

Since we never outgrow our need for human touch, establishing physical contact with your child from birth on will be as beneficial to you as it is to your child. It is a simple and effective way for fathers, in particular, to bond with the baby and become more involved in childcare. In short, touch and regular physical contact is important for the physical and mental health of infants, children, and adults of all ages.

Massaging, stroking, cuddling, hugging, petting, patting, or even just running your fingers through your child's hair tell your child, at the deepest level, that he is loved and that he is safe and secure. Gently massaging your child as he lies in bed is a lovely way to strengthen the bonds of love between you and your child. Massage is also a perfect way to relax your child's body and mind. A back rub with a little lavender-scented oil is a great way to end your child's day.

Be sure to touch, hold, cuddle, kiss, and hug before saying "good night." The classical physical demonstrations of a parent's love for a child are enormously important. So many people of our parents' generation were wrongly told that holding a child was bad and that it would "spoil" the child. Many parents today are the products of such affection-starved childhoods. Our parents had the best intentions but the worst advice. Our parents may have loved us deeply and wanted the very best for us, but the advice they were given on how to nurture their children was non-nurturing and counterproductive. As a result of such child-raising practices, it may be hard and even uncomfortable for today's parents to hold, hug, and kiss their children. It is easy to see why it is important that parents overcome their inhibitions in this area. Children need physical affection and bodily contact with their parents and other loved ones. Touch is vitally important for your child's mental health and inner security.

It is especially important for fathers to lavish uninhibited physical affection on their sons. Roughhousing is not enough. Limiting your contact with your son to organized competitive sports is an especially cruel form of emotional blackmail. Watching television together is not a form of quality time sharing, either. Boys desperately need comforting body contact and generous displays of physical affection from their fathers. An affection-starved child will not grow up to be an emotionally healthy or secure adult. Holding, hugging, cuddling, kissing, and massaging your child are as beneficial to the parent as to the child. Although physical affection should not be limited to bedtime, this is an ideal time for this healthy contact to take place.

Physical affection is also extremely important for adopted children. Even if they were placed in the arms of their adoptive mother immediately after birth, at a deep level, some adopted children may be affected by the separation from their biological mother. It may not seem so serious to adult observers, but to the infant or child, the separation from the birth mother may be incomprehensible and traumatic. Some adopted infants and children may need more physical affection and reassurances than children living with their biological parents. It is important to give adopted children as much affection as they require. Their heightened need for human contact can often be especially apparent at bedtime. Whether your children are adopted or biologically "the fruit of your loins," hold them, massage them, and lavish on them all the love you have in you.

Planning for Tomorrow

As your child lies in bed, quietly make plans with him for the next day's pleasurable activities. Even if he is just going to school, as he does every weekday, gently and positively tell him what a good day he will have. Without being the least bit pedantic, tell him how important the next day's lessons will be. Tell him how lucky he is to go to school, and how lucky you are to have him as your child. Even if your child is not yet in school, reinforce the message that tomorrow will be a good day. Be sure to emphasize in a sincere and enthusiastic manner that learning is fun. Even if your older child's homework was not finished by bedtime, be calm and relaxed.

Reassure your child that there is absolutely nothing in the world to worry about, that everything will be taken care of as long as you love each other. Homework can always be finished the next morning before school, if necessary. Even an unpleasant day marred by unhappy experiences should close with positive thinking and planning for the immediate and distant future. Always close your planning session with a summary of the accomplishments to be made the next day.

It does not really matter what you say at this special time before sleep, as long as your words are positive, supportive, and loving. The underlying message is that you love your child and that she is important to you. No matter how old she is, your child will hear this underlying message. These reassurances are vital to your child's emotional well-being. Frequent verbal reminders and physical demonstrations of your love will help your child become secure, balanced, self-assured, and confident. Let her know that you are always there for her.

One mother tells me that the most effective ritual for helping her daughter relax and fall asleep is talking about tomorrow. This wonderful mother emphasizes what a great day tomorrow will be, and this makes her daughter so happy and secure that, in fact, tomorrow, when it comes, usually is a great day. The effectiveness of this ritual is probably not so much the psychological suggestion, but the state of security and peace that it brings to the child. This feeling enables the child to sleep peacefully and deeply. She wakes up in the morning feeling refreshed and rested, and we all know how great it is to wake up feeling like that.

The Benefits of an Occasional Warm Drink at Bedtime

Sometimes, restlessness prevents a child from relaxing enough to fall asleep. On these occasions, a warm cup of chamomile tea is one old-fashioned remedy for restlessness that many parents swear by. Taken without sweeteners, a small, soothing cup or even just a few sips of chamomile tea can help both parent and child relax. Science has not yet investigated whether chamomile really contains any specific sleep-inducing agents, but the lovely aroma, the warmth of the tea, and the gracious intimacy of quietly sharing a small pot of tea definitely have a beneficial psychological effect. Black tea and Japanese green tea, however, contain caffeine and should be avoided at all costs. Indeed, the importance of children avoiding beverages that contain caffeine cannot be too strongly emphasized.

I do not recommend hot or warm milk or hot cocoa at bedtime. Commercially available hot cocoa drinks are filled with chemicals, sugar, and additives. Even by itself, cocoa has enough caffeine to disrupt a child's sleep. Although infants thrive on mother's milk and generally fall asleep after nursing, cow's milk or any other nonhuman animal milk before bed is not the same thing, especially for older children. Cow's milk, even though it contains tryptophan—a sleep-inducing amino acid—requires prolonged digestion and, among other reasons, is therefore not compatible with restful sleep.

The amount of chamomile tea consumed at bedtime is best limited to a minimal amount simply because the consumption of liquids will usually necessitate urination during the night. No one enjoys being awakened in the middle of the night by a full bladder, and your child is no exception. For the same reason, a glass of water at bedtime is best avoided. Still, some children, especially on hot nights, may want a glass of water to be placed by their bed at night so that they can sip as needed. This is probably all right, but I suspect that the need to drink water at night could sometimes be a physiological reaction to an uncomfortably high salt intake. Of course, if one has consumed too much salt, it is necessary to drink more water than usual, but I think we can all agree that it would be better to avoid the salt in the first place.

These are just a few ideas for rituals that will be useful in helping your child go to sleep. You and your children may evolve others that are more appropriate for your family. The most important thing is for parents to reinforce the idea that bedtime is a positive time. Bedtime should never be associated with punishment or abandonment. Many children resist going to bed because they have learned to associate bedtime and sleep with abandonment, deprivation, and punishment. Engaging in these rituals will make your child feel safe, secure, and loved, and a child who has these feelings instilled in him will have a greater chance to grow up to be a happy, well-adjusted, independent, responsible adult. This is, after all, one of the important jobs of a parent. The benefits to be gained by spending a little quality time with your children engaging in positive bedtime rituals will mean that both you and your children are more likely to get a good night's sleep and awaken the next morning feeling refreshed, invigorated, and prepared to have a successful day.

Chapter 7

The Co-Sleeping Question

$\mathcal{F}$or most of human history and in most human societies today, parents sleep with their children. The natural setting for infant sleep is co-sleeping in the safety, security, and warmth of the arms of parents or other loved ones. This is the environment within which infant sleep evolved over at least five million years of human evolution. Indeed, most baby mammals sleep snuggled up against their mother or father. Even some species of snakes sleep coiled up against their mothers as babies and in large communities as adults.

Solitary sleeping in infancy is a very recent custom that is limited to some Western industrialized societies. It is unsurprising, then, that most American families are unfamiliar with the concept of co-sleeping. Some people might even imagine that co-sleeping is just something done by poor people or people who do not know any better. I can reassure you, though, that, throughout the world, families who co-sleep do not do so because they do not know any better or because their economic circumstances prevent them from having separate beds. They do so because it is the most obvious sleeping arrangement for mother and infant. This is a bit of human wisdom that was largely forgotten in middle-class American society for several generations. Today, it is being rediscovered and is becoming increasingly mainstream.

Co-sleeping, like breast-feeding, is on the rise among middle-class white families. It has always been more common among minority families,[1,2] who neither had the money to buy misguided childcare books nor the inclination to buy them in the first place. In minority families, more traditional family structures still prevailed.

Traditional wisdom has always known that, under the right circumstances, sleeping with your child is simply the most effective way of helping your child get a good night's sleep. Sleeping with your child demonstrates to your child how to sleep. Babies and children, after all, are in a perpetual mode of learning and socialization. Letting your baby observe your sleeping patterns informs him what his future sleeping patterns will be.

Bed sharing may be the most natural thing to do with your baby, but, like so many natural behaviors, it has many real benefits that science is just beginning to document. Many parents are very interested to learn, for instance, that studies have shown that children who sleep with adults are at a significantly lower risk of sudden infant death syndrome (SIDS).[3,4] Even just sharing a bedroom with your child, without necessarily sleeping in the same bed, is protective against SIDS.[5]

There are also important psychological benefits to co-sleeping. It can effortlessly strengthen the bond of love between parent and child. It can foster in your child a powerful sense of security and self-assurance. Co-sleeping can also be important in helping your child develop into a loving, balanced, self-confident, self-reliant, independent person. Researcher James J. McKenna, professor of anthropology and director of the distinguished Mother-Baby Behavioral Sleep Laboratory at the University of Notre Dame, has confirmed the importance of parent/child co-sleeping in his many studies and publications.[6] Professor McKenna cites important medical research demonstrating that adults who, during their childhood, co-slept with their parents are more likely to be more secure, have greater self-esteem, and be more independent and self-reliant.[7] These are goals that all good parents want for their children. Why, then, has co-sleeping become such a contentious issue in middle-class American society?

A Short History of Co-Sleeping and Childcare in America

Interestingly enough, co-sleeping used to be the norm in all levels of American society in the nineteenth century. In most middle- and upper-class families, for instance, children slept in the same bed with their nurses and nannies. The advantages of this arrangement were considered to be so self-evident as to be beyond question. During the Depression of the 1930s and the subsequent Cold War era, however, sociological anxieties and industrial pressures brought a great number of changes to American society. Traditional family life was questioned, and efforts were made to "modernize" and "sanitize" our lives.

As it turns out, not all of these changes were for the good, and few of these changes were good for infants and children. For instance, for most of human history, birth had been considered a normal biological event that took place in the comfort and safety of the home. After being born, a baby was put to the breast, and it stayed with the mother, protected in her loving embrace.

In the middle of the twentieth century, however, birth was radically transformed into a "medical emergency," one that suddenly seemed to require a panicked ride to the hospital in an ambulance, the intervention of masked medical "experts," the introduction of invasive surgical procedures, the injection of drugs, the imposition of a lengthy convalescence in the hospital, and the complete separation of the baby from her mother, except perhaps for a few brief, supervised visits during the day. Under bright fluorescent lights, babies were stored in vast, sterile hospital "nurseries." They were tightly swaddled and kept in individual plastic boxes so that masked hospital staff could perform their systematic, factory-style procedures. Instead of nestling in their mother's arms, babies were routinely jabbed with needles, prodded, and poked with cold, stainless-steel instruments. Instead of the warm and comforting continuous nourishment of the mother's breast, babies were fed artificial, factory-made formulas administered through plastic bottles, on a restrictive and heavily regimented schedule that was organized more for the convenience of the institution than for the baby's true physiological needs. Instead of hearing the mother's heartbeat and the soft cooing and singing of her voice, a newborn baby's ears were constantly filled with the cacophonous din created by the screaming and wailing of other babies, punctuated by the jarring tones of angry nurses barking orders to hospital staff.

Many male babies in the United States, if born in a typical urban hospital, suffered the additional torment, terror, and humiliation of having the end of their penis surgically amputated—without any form of pain relief! Obviously, the constant, agonizing pain caused by the surgical wound on the penis was hardly conducive to restful sleep. The institutionalization of this senseless surgery, called circumcision, provides the clearest evidence of the intense psychosexual anxieties that characterized this era. The creation of medical-sounding "studies" to support this anti-child practice and reduce parents to a state of nonresistance was motivated by the same societal forces that sought to create "medical" studies to enforce the separation of mother from child, to discourage breast-feeding, and to discourage responding to a baby's cries.[8]

For many parents of this era, birth was no longer an occasion for joy and family cooperation but one of fear, pain, and confusion. Similarly, childcare became a great mystery to parents. Whereas in the past, several generations lived in the same house and transmitted childcare knowledge by sharing in the childcare duties, now, new parents, living by themselves, had no one to turn to except the many childcare books on the market. Many of these books reflected the anxieties of the time. Parents were advised never to pick up their babies. They were instructed to let babies cry and to restrict feeding to systematized schedules. Artificial feeding was promoted, and breast-feeding was discouraged as being "unsafe" and "backward." As part of this hostile attitude toward children—an attitude that attempted to minimize all physical contact between parent and child—

co-sleeping was condemned as "dirty," "unhygienic," and "psychologically damaging." There were no objective scientific studies to support these views, but they were believed nonetheless.

It is a wonder that anyone survived such harsh, inhumane treatment at the most vulnerable time of life. The fact that so many people did survive, apparently unscathed, however, does not vindicate or justify this cruel system. We must not fall into the self-defeating trap of thinking that just because we are the products of such a system, our own children should be subjected to it as well. Instead, we should learn from the mistakes of the past in order to give to our own children all the advantages we were denied.

Parents should want their children to have a better life than they had, even if the parents are not convinced that they suffered any sort of deprivation. It is only natural to want the best for your child. After all, we do not want to be a nation of "survivors," but a nation of *champions*, who have been blessed by having the benefits of the most loving, nurturing, and supportive childhood possible. Thankfully, we are today witnessing the gradual disappearance of these unhealthy and negative practices. Our society is becoming increasingly child-friendly. There is still a lot of progress to be made, but I believe we are on the road to success.

Why Do Some Doctors Think That Co-Sleeping Is Dangerous?

Many of you will remember the alarming headlines that appeared in newspapers in the fall of 1999 about a new "study" that prompted the federal Consumer Product Safety Commission to issue a warning that parents should not sleep in the same bed with a baby or toddler under age two because of the alleged risks it poses to the baby.[9] Dr. James J. McKenna, director of the University of Notre Dame Mother-Baby Behavioral Sleep Laboratory, called this report "one of the scientifically less substantial papers that I've seen."[10] The "study" was not a study in the normal sense of the word, but just a collection and tabulation of the results of a few selected studies.[11] The newspaper reports of this study ignored crucial information that parents should have been given.

It is true that a very small number of babies have died while sleeping with their parents, but the cause and circumstances of the death are the most important factors, rather than the fact of the death. In almost every case of a baby dying while sleeping with a parent, it has been shown that the bed was inappropriate for a baby, and the parent was either a smoker, or was drunk, obese, on medication, on drugs, or a combination of these.[12] Further associated risk factors are mattresses that are too soft and waterbeds or beds that are so poorly constructed that they allow a baby to get wedged between the mattress and the wall, headboard, or an adjacent piece of furniture. All of these factors are avoidable. When provided with the important facts, parents who want to co-sleep can make the appropriate changes to their bedroom so that this category of risk can be eliminated.

Although some babies have died while co-sleeping with irresponsible adults, it is important to remember that a far greater number of babies have died while sleeping alone. In most cases of SIDS, lack of supervision at the time of death is the most common feature.[13] Also, it is often impossible to distinguish between suffocation and SIDS. We simply cannot say that there is a single cause of SIDS. It is mostly likely that there are multiple causes.

Some people claim that co-sleeping increases the risk of SIDS. What they fail to realize is that studies consistently show that there is a slight increase in SIDS only for co-sleeping babies whose mothers smoke.[14–18] Clearly, the real problem was that the baby had either an irresponsible mother, or a mother who somehow was not made aware of the dangers of smoking. Co-sleeping itself is not the problem.

Objective studies consistently show that as long as the parent is a responsible nonsmoker, and as long as the mattress is firm and fits perfectly, and as long as the baby sleeps on his back, co-sleeping is not only perfectly safe but also safer than solitary sleeping. Co-sleeping allows parents to monitor the baby to make sure that he is not sleeping on his abdomen, which is strongly associated with SIDS.

It is tragic that any babies have died while co-sleeping, but in every case where all the facts have been reported, the death was the result of avoidable accident or parental irresponsibility. Co-sleeping is the most natural and lovely thing, but, like everything a parent does with a baby, it must be done with care, intelligence, responsibility, and common sense.

Safety Tips for Co-Sleeping

Here are some safety tips for sleeping with your child:

- Make sure that your mattress is firm and fits tightly in the frame. There should be no cutouts in the headboard or footboard. No waterbeds.
- Babies should not be overwrapped or have their heads covered by blankets.
- Neither of the parents should smoke, take drugs, be obese, or be on medication.
- Neither of the parents or anyone else who sleeps with the child should drink alcohol. Even one glass of wine or beer makes you a potential danger to your child.
- Babies should never lie face-down or be allowed to sleep on pillows.
- Parents should seek a doctor's advice if the baby has a fever.

The Benefits of Co-Sleeping

Many cultures, such as the Japanese, hold the charming belief that babies are simply too little to sleep alone. Babies should sleep beside their mother. There is strong scientific support for these folk beliefs. Research shows that co-sleeping has the interesting effect of regulating the infant's breathing patterns and body temperature in a healthy way. For instance, bed sharing is associated with a significantly increased mean axillary temperature compared to solitary sleeping, with the increase expressed only in non-REM sleep, there being no differences during REM sleep or waking.[19] Deep body temperature of infants who co-sleep is also higher than among infants who sleep alone.[20] One study, which compared Asian and white infants, found that Asian infants had similar body temperature patterns to white infants but tended to develop the adultlike pattern later, not earlier as might have been expected.[21] The reason is that more Asian infants than white infants in the study sample slept with their parents, and, before the adultlike body temperature patterns appeared, co-sleeping infants had higher body temperatures than those sleeping alone in their own cots. Not surprisingly, Asian infants are less likely to suffer cot death. This study underscores the important physiological and developmental fact that infants do not normally display the same sleep patterns as adults, and, consequently, their differing physiology should be respected rather than fought against.

The bed-sharing environment can have a significant impact on respiratory control in the infant. Evidence also suggests that routine bed sharing may result in subtle neurophysiological and/or developmental differences in infants. For instance, dangerous episodes of sleep apnea—a condition in which babies simply stop breathing—are greatly reduced when the baby regularly sleeps with its mother.[22]

It is interesting to learn that, in contrast to the widespread belief that having a child in the bed results in loss of sleep for parents, studies show just the opposite result.[23] There is a slight increase in arousals, but, on the whole, nocturnal wakefulness is not increased. The critically important amount of rapid eye movement (REM) sleep is unaffected by co-sleeping. From the baby's perspective, the effect that co-sleeping has on maternal sleep is beneficial because the opportunities for the mother to monitor the baby's status are enhanced. For babies, there is an increase in nighttime arousals, but this is most likely an important protective response during sleep. Indeed, the decrease in the number of arousals during solitary sleeping is hypothesized to play a role in the etiology of SIDS.[24] Co-sleeping is also characterized by a remarkable synchronicity in infant and maternal arousals, meaning that co-sleeping mothers and babies spend more time at the same sleep or wakefulness levels.[25,26] This is precisely the environment in which the hominid infant's sleep, breathing, and arousal patterns evolved.[27] From the evolutionary perspective, then, we can see that nocturnal separation is an alien experience for both babies and mothers and has severe implications for maternal and infant well-being in general and SIDS in particular.

Co-sleeping permits the child to enjoy the security and safety of body contact with her mother throughout the night and permits her to breast-feed whenever she needs to, without crying. Likewise, babies who co-sleep are more likely to be breast-fed for longer individual feeding sessions and over a longer period of time.[28] While sleeping in the same bed, mothers nurse their infants three times more frequently than they do if their infants sleep in a different room.[29] We can all agree that there are no benefits to denying babies the unmatchable nourishment of mother's milk.

One of the important factors in co-sleeping is the orientation of mother to baby. The most frequent pattern seen is a face-to-face arrangement. One study found that while sleeping in a face-to-face orientation, most mother/infant pairs slept most of the time less than 30 centimeters apart, and much of the time less than 20 centimeters.[30] The authors of the study hypothesize that this orientation and closeness facilitate sensory exchanges between mother and baby, which may influence the baby's sleep physiology and nocturnal behavior. Furthermore, the significant percentage of the night that mothers spend oriented toward their baby makes possible a higher degree of maternal vigilance.

As I have mentioned above, an important and authoritative study found that boys who co-slept between the ages of six and eleven had higher self-esteem than boys who did not.[31] We can deduce from this that co-sleeping can foster a more independent, self-assured, confident, self-reliant, and intimate adult with higher self-esteem. Since one of the goals of good parenting is to foster these positive qualities, co-sleeping is obviously one of the best and easiest ways to achieve this goal.

If your child needs the security and comfort of co-sleeping, support that need and find a loving and compassionate way to meet it. You will find that sleeping with your child is as natural and as simple as I have described it. It may be hard for you at first, but as you overcome the anxieties fostered by the negative child-rearing practices that you may have experienced in your own childhood, you will find that sleeping with your child is comfortable and reassuring for you as well. Not only will you have the security of knowing that your child is safe and secure, but your child will also know it and will be much less likely to cry during the night.

I should mention that not all children want to co-sleep. If your child always prefers to sleep alone, support that preference. Even those children who do express a need to co-sleep generally only do so for a few years. Often around age four or five, formerly co-sleeping children may express a desire to sleep by themselves in their own bed. This desire should be supported lovingly. On occasion, older children may want to sleep with their parents or another responsible person, such as grandparents or older siblings. This desire should also be lovingly supported.

Having More Than One Child in the Bed

Since the incidence of multiple births is on the rise, many parents wonder whether co-sleeping is possible or desirable with two or more babies. I can reassure you that sleeping with twins is certainly possible and has the same advantages as sleeping with a single infant. Both babies will benefit by being close to the parents at night, especially during nursing sessions. Having twins is certainly more work than having a single baby, but having your twins sleep apart from you does not lessen the amount of work.

On a similar note, parents who already co-sleep with a youngster wonder what they should do when a newborn baby comes into their lives. Should the older child be encouraged to sleep alone in his own room to make room for the baby?

The introduction of a new baby into the household can sometimes be difficult for children. They can be especially vulnerable in this situation. The best thing you can do is include your older child in the experience.

Give your child every reassurance that you still love and cherish him. Let him know that he is still part of the family and part of the family bed.

Since children sleep so soundly, it is very unlikely that your child will be disturbed by any of the newborn baby's night wakings, but if he should be disturbed, ask him very gently if he would like to try sleeping in another room for a while. Leave the decision up to your child and support whatever decision he makes. Be certain to let him know that he is welcome to come back into the family bed whenever he chooses.

Some younger children in this situation may even want to breast-feed just like the newborn baby. There is no harm in this. It is usually just a sign that your child is feeling insecure and vulnerable. What he really wants is the reassurance that you still love him. If the simple and beautiful act of breast-feeding can give your child the reassurance that he so desperately needs, then the best way to help your child overcome these feelings is to let him breast-feed. Remember to be loving, cheerful, gracious, caring, and above all *flexible* with your older child. Treat him with the same amount of compassion that you would have enjoyed at his age and in his situation.

Common Concerns About Co-Sleeping

Many parents have legitimate questions about co-sleeping. Here are some of their concerns.

Privacy

Having your child in your bed certainly does affect matters of privacy and personal space. Some parents, for instance, feel that they need time away from their children. There is nothing wrong with this. We all need time alone to refresh ourselves. Co-sleeping may not always be the best arrangement for either you or your children, especially if you have a highly developed need for privacy.

For most parents, however, sleeping with their baby or with their younger children is no more an invasion of privacy than sleeping with a spouse. Sleeping with another person of any age generally means going through a period of adaptation. If you want to co-sleep with your new-born baby, remember that the frequent night wakings and the extra vigilance that you experience would still be present if your baby slept apart from you. Your maternal instincts will inevitably be just as strong regardless of sleeping arrangements.

Sufficient Sleep

Some parents believe, and usually correctly, that they would not get any sleep with a child in their bed. Children can move around during the night. Having just gotten used to sleeping with a spouse, the prospect of going through the process again by having to accustom oneself to sleeping with a child can seem like an unwelcome and unnecessary burden for parents who themselves have sleep problems. Some parents who suffer from sleep disorders fear that having a child in bed with them will exacerbate their condition. They may be right, but banishing a child from the parent's bed will not solve the parent's sleep problems. If you do have sleep problems yourself, address them sensibly and, if necessary, seek the counsel of a sleep specialist.

Parental Sexual Intimacy

Many parents are very concerned that having a child in their bed will mean an end to their sex life. Some parents fear that their lovemaking patterns are too inflexible to withstand any alteration. They may not trust themselves to discover ways of increasing the flexibility of their amorous needs. I can assure you, though, that in families that co-sleep, satisfactory solutions are discovered and enjoyed. Many parents in this situation report that their lovemaking has actually benefited and been enriched by their having to be inventive. Being alert for opportunities to make love when such opportunities arise has, for many parents, increased, improved, sustained, and prolonged their sex life.

The key to maintaining a satisfactory and healthy sex life even in a co-sleeping family situation requires that parents be honest with their children about sex. Parents in co-sleeping families will only experience problems if they try to hide the facts of life from their children. If you are honest and open about sex with your children, they will be understanding.

Children are never too young to learn the facts of life. When you tell them, be sure to stress, though, that sex is not just about making babies. Your children, whatever their age, will understand when you tell them that sex is also one of the ways that adults express their love for each other. Your children may think that you are very silly for expressing love in this way, but I am sure that you are mature enough to handle the reproving glance of a child with grace and forbearance.

Children usually have a healthy interest in sex, but, at the same time, they typically have little patience for "mushy" scenes. Witness how they turn up their noses with bemused disbelief at the "silliness" of adults in kissing scenes in movies or on television.

For instance, the little children in one co-sleeping family that I know have been raised in a very enlightened atmosphere. Like many children in co-sleeping families, they have developed strategies for handling their parents when they detect that the parents have fallen into an amorous mood. At the first sign of heightened affection, the children say to their parents: "Yuck, you two need to go on a date!" With an air of authority, superiority, and amusement, the children march out of the bedroom and go play elsewhere in the house.

Other parents I know enjoy the benefits of co-sleeping with their children and have sex on weekend afternoons when the children are off playing at a friend's home. They take advantage of opportunities that arise when the children spend the night at friends' homes. Sometimes they come home from work early, long before the children get home from school, and use the time productively. Co-sleeping with their children has not hampered their sex life in the least.

The parents in yet another co-sleeping family that I know have honestly acknowledged to themselves that they really do not want sex as much as they did in the early days of their marriage. Still, they are very romantic with each other. By being open and honest, they have found that their marriage bond has been strengthened. The opportunity to sleep and snuggle with each other and with their children in bed brings them more joy than the unlimited opportunity to have sex would. This creative couple still has sex, but they make it special by occasionally putting the children to bed early and having a "date" at home: a romantic candlelit dinner, soft music, and then passionate lovemaking in front of a log fire. When the date has come to a romantic close, they quietly slip back to the family bedroom and snuggle in with the children.

We must also acknowledge that even parents who do not co-sleep with their children and maintain a private adults-only bedroom have to be just as thoughtful, creative, and inventive if they want to maintain a healthy sex life. Rigidly clinging to the idea that sex can only take place in the parental bed at nighttime is a sure recipe for marital problems. Stagnation, inflexibility, and routine are among the most common causes of loss of sexual interest and intimacy between partners. One of the benefits of the family bed is that it requires parents who want to maintain an active sex life to remain flexible, creative, and alert. This can only strengthen the marital bond.

Insecurity About Incest

Some parents may fear that co-sleeping might be misinterpreted by others as a form of incest. Sadly, where incestual compulsions exist, separate sleeping arrangements have never been a deterrent. Conversely, sleeping in the same bed with a child cannot induce a mentally balanced parent to commit incest.

The extensive medical literature on this topic has never identified co-sleeping as a risk factor for incest. Incest is usually a symptom of severe mental problems and is usually associated with alcoholism, domestic violence, and other types of physical and mental abuse.[32–36] If you and your spouse are free of mental problems, incest will not be an issue. If you suspect that either you or your spouse do have inappropriate compulsions, please get help immediately.

In general, though, I think we can all agree that it is a mistake to concern oneself with what others might think. We cannot control what other people think; therefore, we should not let our fears about their thoughts control our lives. Our first priority is to our children. Besides, no right-thinking person would confuse co-sleeping with incest. Similarly, no right-thinking person would confuse healthy physical affection with incest.

Babies need constant physical contact with their parents. Bare-skin contact is the very best of all. Children of all ages need physical contact and generous displays of physical affection from their parents and other loved ones. Because the need for such contact is vitally important for your child, parents who are struggling with fears over incest would do themselves and their children an enormous service by seeking competent psychiatric or psychological counseling. The psychological health of our babies and children should not be sacrificed because of the easily allayed fears and confusions from which some parents may suffer.

Insecurities About Public Displays of Affection

Some parents may also be uncomfortable displaying physical affection for each other in front of a child. They may believe that children will be harmed by seeing their parents being loving to each other. No scientific research supports such a belief, but obviously any parent who harbors such a belief would be wise to seek counseling. I believe that children benefit from observing their parents being affectionate with each other. It gives them a positive view of committed relationships and demonstrates to them the beauty and power of love.

Usually such inhibitions are a symptom of deep-seated insecurities that can be successfully addressed in therapy. Obviously, there is a healthy balance between inhibition and exhibitionism. I am confident that all intelligent, confident, and mentally balanced parents will instinctively know when the display of their physical affection would be better continued in private.

General Psychological Discomfort

In general, if you find that you are simply uncomfortable with the idea of having your child sleep in your bed, you should examine your own feelings very carefully. Ask yourself why you are uncomfortable. What issues and anxieties do the idea of co-sleeping trigger? A father, for instance, may be unhappy with the idea of bringing a baby into the parents' bed because, deep down, he harbors the insecurity that a baby will drive a wedge between him and his wife. The issue of fathers feeling "left out" is very important and should be addressed with seriousness and compassion. It may be helpful to reassure fathers that the baby is sleeping with him just as much as with the mother, even though, obviously, only she can breast-feed the baby. Every effort should be made to ensure that fathers are as deeply involved as mothers.

I suspect that, sometimes, vague anxieties over co-sleeping may also be the result of an emotionally deprived and affection-starved childhood. Childcare books and generalized advice books of the Cold War–era advocated raising children in such an atmosphere. Rather than repeat the unfortunate cycle of emotional deprivation, work out your problems with a competent and informed therapist. It is important not to make your child a martyr to your problems. If your problems are not emotional but are related to sleep problems of your own, then by all means seek medical advice for your own sake. Sleep problems for adults, as well as for children, can be solved. No one need suffer. Any reasonable and loving parent would agree that simply depriving a child of the security and reassurance of sleeping with a responsible adult is not a solution.

Even if the process of uncovering, addressing, and solving anxieties about co-sleeping does not result in you sleeping with your child, the healing process will be of great benefit to you. You may find that the idea of co-sleeping is not really the problem. It may merely be the trigger for deeper issues. No one deserves to go through life burdened with problems of any kind, so please do yourself a favor and find a rational solution. Therapy is only one option.

Let me stress that I am not advocating therapy so that you will sleep with your child. I am advocating therapy for those who would benefit from it for their own sake. Ultimately, your child and all your family members and friends will benefit from your finding greater inner harmony and balance.

Psychological Environment

Although the medical literature is clear that co-sleeping is healthier for the child—assuming that the parents are responsible and that the sleeping environment is safe—it is probably better, I think, that a child should sleep alone in her own bed than be grudgingly taken into a parents' bed that is filled with resentment and inhospitality. The point of co-sleeping is to foster better sleep patterns and strengthen the bond of intimacy between parent and child. If co-sleeping does not produce better sleep patterns and strains the bond of love between parent and child, then co-sleeping, in this instance, is best avoided. Being emotional creatures, children can feel when they are unwelcome or unwanted. No child should be made to feel this way. All interactions between parent and child should be filled with the spirit of love, trust, generosity, and acceptance.

Unfamiliarity with Co-Sleeping

It would be a mistake to categorize parents who will not co-sleep as selfish or unloving. I would like to think that parents who feel that they cannot sleep with their child are just being honest about their own needs and limitations and have made their decision in the best interest of their child.

Most parents, however, do not harbor any feelings of discomfort. They simply have never considered co-sleeping. This is not because they feel it would be an unwelcome intrusion, but because the concept is unfamiliar.

Some parents may not even be aware that co-sleeping is a viable option for fostering good sleeping habits. Some of these parents might have read in the newspapers or in some old-fashioned childcare manuals that co-sleeping is unhealthy or dangerous. The good news that I would like to share is that, with a minimum of commonsense precautions, co-sleeping is as safe and satisfying as sleep gets.

Chapter 8

A Step-by-Step Guide to Fostering Good Sleep Patterns

*T*his chapter contains a step-by-step summary of the most important points covered in this book. I hope that you will find this a useful guide both to fostering healthful sleep and to strengthening the bond of love between you and your child.

Children are very sensitive beings. They may not be able to control their emotions with the same skill that most adults exercise, but children compensate for this by being highly intuitive. They will react strongly to the emotional cues that you direct toward them. Therefore, if you nurture a loving, caring, and compassionate attitude toward your child, you will help your child feel more at ease with himself and more confident with his place in the family. You will also be helping him develop into a more stable, independent, confident, and self-reliant being. These are the very qualities that all parents should want for their children.

Cultivating a loving and informed approach to parenting will create the sort of safe, nurturing, and stable environment that your child needs to develop and maintain good sleep habits. It is for this reason that so many of the steps listed here are based on maintaining and improving the relationship between parent and child. The more flexible, relaxed, and loving you become, the more your child will respond with loving, respectful, and cheerful behavior. The more you involve yourself in your child's daily life and routines, the more you will be able to protect your child from the stresses that disrupt sleep. In short, your child's sleep depends on you.

During Babyhood

Step 1. Remind yourself that babies are unable to sleep through the night until they are about three months old. Some babies take longer.

Step 2. Remind yourself that a baby's sleep patterns are different from those of an adult.

Step 3. Remind yourself that your baby is unique and that he will have a different sleep pattern from any other baby.

Step 4. It is okay to sleep with your baby.

Step 5. Nurse your newborn baby whenever she wants to nurse or at least once every two hours.

Step 6. Nursing your baby in bed with you at night is a perfect way of meeting your baby's nutritional needs and fostering good sleep patterns at the same time.

Step 7. If your toddler or young child wants to nurse at night, even after he has weaned himself onto solid foods, support this lovingly. Nursing is just as much about security and love as it is about nourishment.

Step 8. If you do sleep with your baby, take every precaution to make the family bed as safe and secure as possible. Be a responsible parent.

Step 9. If your baby sleeps alone, take every precaution to make your baby's sleep environment as safe and secure as possible. Be a responsible parent.

Step 10. Protect your baby from any stressful experiences that can disrupt sleep in the short term and the long term.

Step 11. Protect your baby from the harmful effects of secondhand tobacco smoke.

Step 12. Whatever the age of your baby, if she wakes up in the night to feed or cuddle, be gentle, calming, and reassuring.

Step 13. Demonstrate to your baby your availability, reliability, dependability, and responsibility.

Step 14. If your baby cries, go to him, pick him up, soothe him, calm him, and solve whatever is bothering him.

Step 15. Never let a baby "cry it out."

Step 16. Love your baby.

Step 17. Take pride in your baby, and take pride in your parenthood.

Step 18. Enjoy every second of being with your precious baby.

Step 19. Lovingly and gratefully accept the individuality of your baby.

Step 20. Lavish love and affection on your baby.

Step 21. Keep your baby with you, next to your body as much as possible.

During Childhood

Step 1. Remind yourself that your child's sleep habits are unique and that they are different from those of an adult or from any other child.

Step 2. Encourage and help your child to adopt the good habits that promote good sleep.

Step 3. See that your child gets plenty of sunshine and exercise each day.

Step 4. See that your child gets a proper nourishing diet every day.

Step 5. Protect your child from the harmful and sleep-disrupting effects of caffeine and junk food.

Step 6. Help your child avoid stressful experiences and activities during the day.

Step 7. Protect your child from any activities, experiences, or procedures that in any way disrupt sleep.

Step 8. Protect your child from the sleep-disrupting effects of television in the evening.

Step 9. Feed your child his evening meal at least two hours before he goes to bed.

Step 10. Be alert for the daytime signs that your child is not getting enough sleep at night: crankiness, drowsiness, slowness waking up in the morning, and so on.

Step 11. Set your child's bedtime early enough so that your child gets as much sleep as she needs to remain alert and cheerful during the day. Most children need at least ten hours of solid sleep.

Step 12. Reflect on the benefit of regular routines, but at all times be flexible and sympathetic.

Step 13. Avoid exposing your child to bright lights in the evening.

Step 14. Make bedtime a special time for togetherness between you and your child.

Step 15. Incorporate positive bedtime rituals into your child's bedtime routine.

Step 16. Encourage your child to go to the bathroom one last time before bed.

Step 17. Make your child's bedroom environment as safe, inviting, calm, and hygienic as possible.

Step 18. Encourage positive behavior by rewarding it.

Step 19. If your child cries, go to him, pick him up, soothe him, calm him, and solve whatever is bothering him.

Step 20. Never let a child "cry it out."

Step 21. Demonstrate to your child your availability, reliability, dependability, and responsibility.

Step 22. If your child wakes up in the night and cries out for you, go to her. Gently and calmly try to reestablish the quiet and calm environment that will help your child fall back asleep.

Step 23. Love your child.

Step 24. Take pride in your child, and take pride in your parenthood.

Step 25. Enjoy every second of being with your precious child.

Step 26. Lovingly and gratefully accept the individuality of your child. No other child is like your child. Accept the child that you have for who he is. Avoid the mistake of trying to turn him into the child you think he ought to be.

Step 27. Lavish love and affection on your child.

During the Teenage Years

Step 1. Remind yourself that teenagers have sleep patterns that are different from those of adults.

Step 2. Remind yourself that teenagers require lots of sleep—sometimes as much as twelve hours a night.

Step 3. Gently encourage your teenager to go to sleep as early as possible on school nights.

Step 4. Avoid discouraging your teenager from sleeping in on weekends or holidays.

Step 5. Remind yourself that growth, development, and puberty take place during sleep in the teenage years.

Step 6. Be sure that your teenager has a nourishing diet.

Step 7. Demonstrate to your teenager your availability, reliability, dependability, and responsibility.

Step 8. Love your teenager.

Step 9. Be sympathetic to the growing pains of the teenage years. Teenagers will make mistakes and say things they do not mean. Learn to forgive and forget.

Step 10. Be as understanding with your teenager as you wish your parents had been with you when you were a teenager.

Step 11. Take pride in your teenager and take pride in your parenthood.

Step 12. Enjoy every second of being with your teenager.

Step 13. Lovingly and gratefully accept the individuality of your teenager.

Step 14. Lavish love and affection on your teenager.

Step 15. Stand by your principles, but be generous with your teenager.

Notes

Chapter 1

1. Scheen A. J., Byrne M. M., Plat L., Leproult R., Van Cauter E. Relationships between sleep quality and glucose regulation in normal humans. *American Journal of Physiology* 1996;271(2 Pt 1):E261–270.

2. Pruessner J. C., Wolf O. T., Hellhammer D. H. Free cortisol levels after awakening: A reliable biological marker for the assessment of adrenocortical activity. *Life Sciences* 1997;61(26):2539–2549.

3. Schmidt-Reinwald A. et al. The cortisol response to awakening in relation to different challenge tests and a 12-hour cortisol rhythm. *Life Sciences* 1999;64(18):1653–1660.

4. Koyanagi T., Horimoto N., Nakano H. REM sleep determined using in utero penile tumescence in the human fetus at term. *Biology of the Neonate* 1991;60 Suppl 1:30–35.

5. Spangler G. The emergence of adrenocortical circadian function in newborns and infants and its relationship to sleep, feeding and maternal adrenocortical activity. *Early Human Development* 1991;25(3):197–208.

6. Larson M. C., White B. P., Cochran A., Donzella B., Gunnar M. Dampening of the cortisol response to handling at 3 months in human infants and its relation to sleep, circadian cortisol activity, and behavioral distress. *Developmental Psychobiology* 1998;33(4):327–337.
7. Polleri A., Masturzo P., Vignola G., Barreca T., Gallamini A. Sleep-wake differences in serum prolactin levels in children. *Journal of Endocrinological Investigation* 1978;1(4):347–350.
8. Antonijevic I. A., Murck H., Frieboes R., Holsboer F., Steiger A. On the gender differences in sleep-endocrine regulation in young normal humans. *Neuroendocrinology* 1999;70(4):280–287.
9. Karacan I., Anch M., Thornby J. I., Okawa M., Williams R. L. Longitudinal sleep patterns during pubertal growth: Four-year follow up. *Pediatric Research* 1975;9(11):842–846.
10. Large D. M., Anderson D. C., Laing I. Twenty-four-hour profiles of serum prolactin during male puberty with and without gynaeco-mastia. *Clinical Endocrinology (Oxford)* 1980;12(3):293–302.
11. Finkelstein J. W., Kapen S., Weitzman E. D., Hellman L., Boyar R. M. Twenty-four-hour plasma prolactin patterns in prepubertal and adolescent boys. *Journal of Clinical Endocrinology and Metabolism* 1978;47(5):1123–1128.
12. Sultan C. et al. [Prolactin secretion during sleep at puberty. Preliminary results.] *Annales de Biologie Clinique (Paris)* 1980;38(3):157–160.
13. Fehm H. L., Clausing J., Kern W., Pietrowsky R., Born J. Sleep-associated augmentation and synchronization of luteinizing hormone pulses in adult men. *Neuroendocrinology* 1991;54(3):192–195.
14. Luboshitzky R., Herer P., Levi M., Shen-Orr Z., Lavie P. Relationship between rapid eye movement sleep and testosterone secretion in normal men. *Journal of Andrology* 1999;20(6):731–737.
15. Strobl J. S., Thomas M. J. Human growth hormone. *Pharmacological Reviews* 1994;46(1):1–34.
16. Carskadon M. A., Harvey K., Duke P., Anders T. F., Litt I. F., Dement W. C. Pubertal changes in daytime sleepiness. *Sleep* 1980;2(4):453–460.

17. Carskadon M. A. Patterns of sleep and sleepiness in adolescents. *Pediatrician* 1990;17(1):5–12.
18. Carskadon M. A., Wolfson A. R., Acebo C., Tzischinsky O., Seifer R. Adolescent sleep patterns, circadian timing, and sleepiness at a transition to early school days. *Sleep*;21(8):871–881(December 15, 1998).
19. Karacan I., Anch M., Thornby J. I., Okawa M., Williams R. L. Longitudinal sleep patterns during pubertal growth: Four-year follow up. *Pediatric Research* 1975;9(11):842–846.
20. Van Cauter E., Plat L. Physiology of growth hormone secretion during sleep. *Journal of Pediatrics* 1996;128(5 Pt 2):S32–37.
21. Guldner J., Schier T., Friess E., Colla M., Holsboer F., Steiger A. Reduced efficacy of growth hormone-releasing hormone in modulating sleep endocrine activity in the elderly. *Neurobiology Aging* 1997;18(5):491–495.
22. Schiavi R. C., Schreiner-Engel P. Nocturnal penile tumescence in healthy aging men. *Journal of Gerontology* 1988;43(5):M146–150.
23. Dijk D. J., Duffy J. F. Circadian regulation of human sleep and age-related changes in its timing, consolidation and EEG character-istics. *Annals of Medicine* 1999;31(2):130–140.
24. Czeisler C. A. et al. Stability, precision, and near-24-hour period of the human circadian pacemaker. *Science*;284(5423):2177–2181(June 25, 1999).
25. Czeisler C. A., Klerman E. B. Circadian and sleep-dependent regulation of hormone release in humans. *Recent Progess in Hormone Research* 1999;54:97–130.
26. Brandenberger G. Symposium: Normal and abnormal REM sleep regulation: Episodic hormone release in relation to REM sleep. *Journal of Sleep Research* 1993;2(4):193–198.
27. Karacan I., Williams R. L., Thornby J. I., Salis P. J. Sleep-related penile tumescence as a function of age. *American Journal of Psychiatry* 1975;132(9):932–937.
28. Hirshkowitz M., Moore C. A. Sleep-related erectile activity. *Neurologic Clinics* 1996;14(4):721–737.

29. Horita H., Kumamoto Y. [Study on nocturnal penile tumescence (NPT) in healthy males study on age-related changes of NPT.] *Nippon Hinyokika Gakkai Zasshi* 1994;85(10):1502–1510.

30. Schiavi R. C. et al. Luteinizing hormone and testosterone during nocturnal sleep: Relation to penile tumescent cycles. *Archives of Sexual Behavior* 1977;6(2):97–104.

31. Leibenluft E. et al. Effects of leuprolide-induced hypogonadism and testosterone replacement on sleep, melatonin, and prolactin secretion in men. *Journal of Clinical Endocrinology and Metabolism* 1997;82(10):3203–3207.

32. Karacan I. et al. Uterine activity during sleep. *Sleep* 1986;9(3): 393–398.

Chapter 2

1. Kataria S., Swanson M. S., Trevathan G. E. Persistence of sleep disturbances in preschool children. *Journal of Pediatrics* 1987; 110(4):642–646.

2. Keener M. A., Zeanah C. H, Anders T. F. Infant temperament, sleep organization, and nighttime parental interventions. *Pediatrics* 1988;81(6):762–771.

3. Named for Richard Ferber, the best-known advocate of this controversial approach. Ferber, Richard. *Solve Your Child's Sleep Problems.* New York: Simon & Schuster, 1986.

4. Ramchandani P., Wiggs L., Webb V., Stores G. A systematic review of treatments for settling problems and night waking in young children. *British Medical Journal*;320(7229):209–213 (January 22, 2000).

5. Kales A. et al. Hereditary factors in sleepwalking and night terrors. *British Journal of Psychiatry* 1980;137:111–118.

6. Llorente M. D., Currier M. B., Norman S. E., Mellman T. A. Night terrors in adults: Phenomenology and relationship to psychopathology. *Journal of Clinical Psychiatry* 1992;53(11): 392–394.

7. Soldatos C. R., Kales A. Sleep disorders: Research in psychopathology and its practical implications. *Acta Psychiatrica Scandinavica* 1982;65(6):381–387.

8. Popoviciu L., Corfariu O. Efficacy and safety of midazolam in the treatment of night terrors in children. *British Journal of Clinical Pharmacology* 1983;16 Suppl 1:97S–102S.

9. Kramer R. L. The treatment of childhood night terrors through the use of hypnosis—a case study: A brief communication. *International Journal of Clinical and Experimental Hypnosis* 1989; 37(4): 283–284.

10. Koe G. G. Hypnotic treatment of sleep terror disorder: A case report. *American Journal of Clinical Hypnosis* 1989;32(1):36–40.

11. Sellinger V. J. Nocturnal enuresis in children. *Lippincott's Primary Care Practice* 1997;1(4):399–407.

12. Hublin C., Kaprio J., Partinen M., Koskenvuo M. Nocturnal enuresis in a nationwide twin cohort. *Sleep*;21(6):579–585 (September 15, 1998).

13. Ward S. L., Marcus C. L. Obstructive sleep apnea in infants and young children. *Journal of Clinical Neurophysiology* 1996;13(3): 198–207.

14. Kahn A. et al. Clinical symptoms associated with brief obstructive sleep apnea in normal infants. *Sleep* 1993;16(5):409–413.

15. Kahn A., Groswasser J., Sottiaux M., Rebuffat E., Franco P. Mechanisms of obstructive sleep apneas in infants. *Biology of the Neonate* 1994;65(3–4):235–239.

16. Mallory G. B. Jr., Fiser D. H., Jackson R. Sleep-associated breathing disorders in morbidly obese children and adolescents. *Journal of Pediatrics* 1989;115(6):892–897.

17. Lee L. Y. et al. Stimulation of vagal pulmonary C-fibers by a single breath of cigarette smoke in dogs. *Journal of Applied Physiology* 1989;66(5):2032–2038.

18. Kahn A. et al. Prenatal exposure to cigarettes in infants with obstructive sleep apneas. *Pediatrics* 1994;93(5):778–783.

19. Toubas P. L. et al. Effects of maternal smoking and caffeine habits on infantile apnea: A retrospective study. *Pediatrics* 1986;78(1):159–163.

20. Alaswad B., Toubas P. L., Grunow J. E. Environmental tobacco smoke exposure and gastroesophageal reflux in infants with apparent life-threatening events. *Journal of the Oklahoma State Medical Association* 1996;89(7):233–237.

21. Leiberman A., Cohen A., Tal A. Digital signal processing of stridor and snoring in children. *International Journal of Pediatric Otorhino-laryngology* 1986;12(2):173–185.

22. Marcus C. L., Hamer A., Loughlin G. M. Natural history of primary snoring in children. *Pediatric Pulmonology* 1998;26(1):6–11.

23. Wang D. Y., Bernheim N., Kaufman L., Clement P. Assessment of adenoid size in children by fibreoptic examination. *Clinical Otolaryngology* 1997;22(2):172–177.

24. McColley S. A. et al. High prevalence of allergic sensitization in children with habitual snoring and obstructive sleep apnea. *Chest* 1997;111(1):170–173.

25. Owen G. O., Canter R. J., Robinson A. Snoring, apnoea and ENT symptoms in the paediatric community. *Clinical Otolaryngology* 1996;21(2):130–134.

26. Gislason T., Benediktsdottir B. Snoring, apneic episodes, and nocturnal hypoxemia among children 6 months to 6 years old. An epidemiologic study of lower limit of prevalence. *Chest* 1995; 107(4):963–966.

27. Clore E. R., Hibel J. The parasomnias of childhood. *Journal of Pediatric Health Care* 1993;7(1):12–16.

28. Kales A. et al. Hereditary factors in sleepwalking and night terrors. *British Journal of Psychiatry* 1980;137:111–118.

29. Masand P., Popli A. P., Weilburg J. B. Sleepwalking. *American Family Physician*;51(3):649–654 (February 15, 1995).

30. Schenck C. H., Mahowald M. W. Review of nocturnal sleep-related eating disorders. *International Journal of Eating Disorders* 1994; 15(4):343–356.

31. Adami G. F., Meneghelli A., Scopinaro N. Night eating and binge eating disorder in obese patients. *International Journal of Eating Disorders* 1999;25(3):335–338.

32. Schenck C. H., Mahowald M. W. Review of nocturnal sleep-related eating disorders. *International Journal of Eating Disorders* 1994; 15(4):343–356.

33. Farrimond T. Sudden infant death syndrome and possible relation to vestibular function. *Perceptual Motor Skills* 1990;71(2):419–423.

34. Jorgensen S., Ronborg S. [The restless leg syndrome]. *Ugeskrift for Laeger*;151(11):670–671 (March 13, 1989).

35. Montplaisir J., Lapierre O., Warnes H., Pelletier G. The treatment of the restless leg syndrome with or without periodic leg movements in sleep. *Sleep* 1992;15(5):391–395.

36. Ring A. et al. Sleep disturbances in children with attention-deficit/ hyperactivity disorder: A comparative study with healthy siblings. *Journal of Learning Disabilities* 1998;31(6):572–578.

37. March J. S. et al. Sertraline in children and adolescents with obsessive-compulsive disorder: A multicenter randomized controlled trial. *Journal of the American Medical Association;* 280(20):1752–1756 (November 25, 1998).

38. Kallepalli B. R. et al. Trazodone is only slightly faster than fluoxetine in relieving insomnia in adolescents with depressive disorders. *Journal of Child Adolescent Psychopharmacology* 1997;7(2): 97–107.

39. Leppik I. E. Antiepileptic drugs in development: Prospects for the near future. *Epilepsia* 1994;35 Suppl 4:S29–40.

40. Richdale A. L, Prior M. R. The sleep/wake rhythm in children with autism. *European Child Adolescent Psychiatry* 1995;4(3):175–186.

41. Stoloff S. W. The changing role of theophylline in pediatric asthma. *American Family Physician* 1994;49(4):839–844.

42. Pelissolo A., Lecendreux M., Mouren-Simeoni M. C. [Use of hypnotics in children: description and analysis.] *Archive of Pediatrics* 1999;6(6):625–630.

43. Minde K. et al. The evaluation and treatment of sleep disturbances in young children. *Journal of Child Psychology and Psychiatry* 1993; 34(4):521–533.

Chapter 3

1. Garfinkel D., Zisapel N., Wainstein J., Laudon M. Facilitation of benzodiazepine discontinuation by melatonin: A new clinical approach. *Archives of Internal Medicine*;159(20):2456–2460. (November 8, 1999).
2. American Academy of Pediatrics, Committee on Communications. Children, adolescents, and television. *Pediatrics* 1990;85(6): 1119–1120.
3. Locard E. et al. Risk factors of obesity in a 5-year-old population: Parental versus environmental factors. *International Journal of Obesity and Related Metabolic Disorders* 1992;16(10):721–729.
4. DuRant R. H., Baranowski T., Johnson M., Thompson W. O. The relationship among television watching, physical activity, and body composition of young children. *Pediatrics* 1994;94(4 Pt 1): 449–455.
5. Gupta R. K. et al. Impact of television on children. *Indian Journal of Pediatrics* 1994;61(2):153–159.
6. Gadow K. D., Sprafkin J. Field experiments of television violence with children: Evidence for an environmental hazard? *Pediatrics* 1989;83(3):399–405.
7. American Academy of Pediatrics, Committee on Communications. Children, adolescents, and television. *Pediatrics* 1990;85(6): 1119–1120.
8. Robinson J. P. Television's impact on everyday life: Some cross-national evidence. In: Rubenstein E. A., Comstock G. A., Murray J. P., eds. *Television and Social Behavior. Television in Day-to-Day Life: Patterns of Use.* Washington, D.C.: Government Printing Office; 1972;4:410–431.
9. Owens J. et al. Television-viewing habits and sleep disturbance in school children. *Pediatrics* 1999;104(3). URL: http:/www.pediatrics. org/cgi/content/full/104/3/e27.

10. Akerstedt T. et al. A 50-Hz electromagnetic field impairs sleep. *Journal of Sleep Research* 1999;8(1):77–81.

11. Sastre A., Cook M. R., Graham C. Nocturnal exposure to intermittent 60 Hz magnetic fields alters human cardiac rhythm. *Bioelectromagnetics* 1998;19(2):98–106.

12. Hatch E. E. et al. Association between childhood acute lympho-blastic leukemia and use of electrical appliances during pregnancy and childhood. *Epidemiology* 1998;9(3):234–245.

13. Green L. M. et al. Childhood leukemia and personal monitoring of residential exposures to electric and magnetic fields in Ontario, Canada. *Cancer Causes & Control* 1999;10(3):233–243.

14. Wartenberg D. Residential magnetic fields and childhood leukemia: A meta-analysis. *American Journal of Public Health* 1998;88(12):1787–1794.

15. Dockerty J. D., Elwood J. M., Skegg D. C., Herbison G. P. Electromagnetic field exposures and childhood cancers in New Zealand. *Cancer Causes & Control* 1998;9(3):299–309.

16. Omura Y., Losco M. Electro-magnetic fields in the home environment (color TV, computer monitor, microwave oven, cellular phone, etc.) as potential contributing factors for the induction of oncogen C-fos Ab1, oncogen C-fos Ab2, integrin alpha 5 beta 1 and development of cancer, as well as effects of microwave on amino acid composition of food and living human brain. *Acupuncture and Electro-Therapeutics Research* 1993;18(1): 33–73.

17. American Academy of Pediatrics, Committee on Public Education. Media Education. *Pediatrics* 1999;104:341–343.

18. Aney M. Babywise's advice linked to dehydration, failure to thrive. *AAP News*;14(4):21 (April 1998).

19. American Academy of Pediatrics, Work Group on Breastfeeding. Statement on breastfeeding and the use of human milk. *Pediatrics* 1997;100(6):1035–1039.

20. Kostoglou-Athanassiou I., Treacher D. F., Wheeler M. J., Forsling M. L. Bright light exposure and pituitary hormone secretion. *Clinical Endocrinology (Oxford)* 1998;48(1):73–79.

21. Boivin D. B., Duffy J. F., Kronauer R. E., Czeisler C. A. Sensitivity of the human circadian pacemaker to moderately bright light. *Journal of Biological Rhythms* 1994;9(3–4):315–331.

22. Taylor J. R., Lockwood A. P., Taylor A. J. The prepuce: Specialized mucosa of the penis and its loss to circumcision. *British Journal of Urology* 1996;77(2):291–295.

23. Winkelmann R. K. The cutaneous innervation of newborn human prepuce. *Journal of Investigative Dermatology* 1956;26(1):53–67.

24. Cold C. J., Taylor J. R. The prepuce. *BJU International* 1999;83 Suppl 1:34–44.

25. Van Howe, R. S. Anaesthesia for circumcision: A review of the literature. In: Denniston G. C., Hodges F. M., Milos M. F., eds. *Male and Female Circumcision: Medical, Legal, and Ethical Considerations in Pediatric Practice.* New York: Kluwer Academic/Plenum Publishers, 1999:67–97.

26. Stern E., Parmelee A. H., Akiyama Y., Schultz M. A., Wenner W. H. Sleep cycle characteristics in infants. *Pediatrics* 1969;43(1):65–70.

27. Gunnar M. R., Fisch R. O., Malone S. The effects of a pacifying stimulus on behavioral and adrenocortical responses to circumcision in the newborn. *Journal of the American Academy of Child Psychiatry* 1984;23(1):34–38.

28. Gunnar M. R., Fisch R. O., Korsvik S., Donhowe J. M. The effects of circumcision on serum cortisol and behavior. *Psychoneuroendocrinology* 1981;6(3):269–275.

29. Anders T. F., Chalemian R. J. The effects of circumcision on sleep-wake states in human neonates. *Psychosomatic Medicine* 1974; 36(2):174–179.

30. Emde R. N., Harmon R. J., Metcalf D., Koenig K. L., Wagonfeld S. Stress and neonatal sleep. *Psychosomatic Medicine* 1971;33(6): 491–497.

31. Marshall R. E. et al. Circumcision: II. Effects upon mother-infant interaction. *Early Human Development* 1982;7(4):367–374.

32. Dixon S., Snyder J., Holve R., Bromberger P. Behavioral effects of

circumcision with and without anesthesia. *Journal of Developmental and Behavioral Pediatrics* 1984;5(5):246–250.

33. Brackbill Y. Continuous stimulation and arousal level in infancy: Effects of stimulus intensity and stress. *Child Development* 1975; 46(2):364–369.

34. Gunnar M. R., Fisch R. O., Malone S. The effects of a pacifying stimulus on behavioral and adrenocortical responses to circumcision in the newborn. *Journal of the American Academy of Child Psychiatry* 1984;23(1):34–38.

35. Gunnar M. R., Malone S., Vance G., Fisch R. O. Coping with aversive stimulation in the neonatal period: Quiet sleep and plasma cortisol levels during recovery from circumcision. *Child Development* 1985;56(4):824–834.

36. Stang H. J. et al. Beyond dorsal penile nerve block: A more humane circumcision. *Pediatrics* 1997;100(2):e3. URL: http://www.pediatrics.org/cgi/content/full/100/2/e3.

37. Williamson P. S., Evans N. D. Neonatal cortisol response to circumcision with anesthesia. *Clinical Pediatrics (Philadelphia)* 1986;25(8):412–415.

38. Maxwell L. G., Yaster M., Wetzel R. C., Niebyl J. R. Penile nerve block for newborn circumcision. *Obstetrics and Gynecology* 1987; 70(3):415–419.

39. Stang H. J. et al. Local anesthesia for neonatal circumcision. *Journal of the American Medical Association*;259(10):1507–1511 (March 11, 1988).

40. Taylor J. R., Lockwood A. P., Taylor A. J. The prepuce: Specialized mucosa of the penis and its loss to circumcision. *British Journal of Urology* 1996;77(2):291–295.

41. Winkelmann R. K. The cutaneous innervation of newborn human prepuce. *Journal of Investigative Dermatology* 1956;26(1):53–67.

42. Taddio A., Goldbach M., Ipp M., Stevens B., Koren G. Effect of neonatal circumcision on pain responses during vaccination in boys. *Lancet*;345(8945):291–292 (February 4, 1995).

43. Taddio A., Katz J., Ilersich A. L., Koren G. Effect of neonatal circumcision on pain response during subsequent routine vaccination. *Lancet*;349(9052):599–603 (March 1, 1997).

44. Marshall R. E. et al. Circumcision: II. Effects upon mother-infant interaction. *Early Human Development* 1982;7(4):367–374.

45. Dixon S., Snyder J., Holve R., Bromberger P. Behavioral effects of circumcision with and without anesthesia. *Journal of Developmental and Behavioral Pediatrics* 1984;5(5):246–250.

46. Howard C. R., Howard F. M., Weitzman M. L. Acetaminophen analgesia in neonatal circumcision: The effect on pain. *Pediatrics* 1994;93(4):641–646.

47. Dixon S., Snyder J., Holve R., Bromberger P. Behavioral effects of circumcision with and without anesthesia. *Journal of Developmental and Behavioral Pediatrics* 1984;5(5):246–250.

48. Weissbluth M., Davis A. T., Poncher J. Night waking in 4- to 8-month–old infants. *Journal of Pediatrics* 1984;104(3):477–480.

49. Anders T. F. Night-waking in infants during the first year of life. *Pediatrics* 1979;63(6):860–864.

50. Goldman, Ronald. *Questioning Circumcision: A Jewish Perspective.* Boston: Vanguard Publications, 1998.

51. Fleiss P. M. The case against circumcision. *Mothering* (Winter 1997):36–45.

52. Caffeine content of popular drinks. http://wilstar.net/caffeine.htm (access date: January 2, 2000).

53. Shively C. A., Tarka S. M. Jr. Methylxanthine composition and consumption patterns of cocoa and chocolate products. *Progress in Clinical and Biological Research* 1984;158:149–178.

54. Feikema W. J. [Headache and chronic sleep deprivation: An often missed relationship in children and also in adults.] *Nederlands Tijdschrift voor Geneeskunde*;143(38):1897–1900 (September 18, 1999).

55. Lin A. S., Uhde T. W., Slate S. O., McCann U. D. Effects of intravenous caffeine administered to healthy males during sleep. *Depression and Anxiety* 1997;5(1):21–28.

56. Wright K. P. Jr., Badia P., Myers B. L., Plenzler S. C., Hakel M. Caffeine and light effects on nighttime melatonin and temperature levels in sleep-deprived humans. *Brain Research*;747(1):78–84 (January 30, 1997).

57. Lee K. A., McEnany G., Weekes D. Gender differences in sleep patterns for early adolescents. *Journal of Adolescent Health* 1999; 24(1):16–20.

58. Roth T., Roehrs T., Koshorek G., Sicklesteel J., Zorick F. Sedative effects of antihistamines. *Journal of Allergy and Clinical Immunology* 1987;80(1):94–98.

59. Sestili M. A. Possible adverse health effects of vitamin C and ascorbic acid. *Seminars in Oncology* 1983;10(3):299–304.

60. Cathcart R. F. Vitamin C, titrating to bowel tolerance, anascorbemia, and acute induced scurvy. *Medical Hypotheses* 1981;7(11): 1359–1376.

Chapter 4

1. Akerstedt T., Arnetz B., Ficca G., Paulsson L. E., Kallner A. A 50-Hz electromagnetic field impairs sleep. *Journal of Sleep Research* 1999;8(1):77–81.

2. Quinn G. E., Shin C. H., Maguire M. G., Stone R. A. Myopia and ambient lighting at night. *Nature*;399(6732):113–114 (May 13, 1999).

3. Mitchell E. A., Scragg L., Clements M. Soft cot mattresses and the sudden infant death syndrome. *New Zealand Medical Journal*; 109(1023):206–207 (June 14, 1996).

4. L'Hoir M. P., et al. Sudden unexpected death in infancy: Epidemiologically determined risk factors related to pathological classification. *Acta Paediatrica* 1998;87(12):1279–1287.

5. Oudesluys-Murphy A. M., van Yperen W. J. The cot in cot deaths. *European Journal of Pediatrics* 1988;147(1):85–86.

6. Brooke H., Gibson A., Tappin D., Brown H. Case-control study of sudden infant death syndrome in Scotland, 1992–5. *British Medical Journal*;314(7093):1516–1520 (May 24, 1997).

7. Gilbert-Barness E. et al. Hazards of mattresses, beds and bedding in deaths of infants. *American Journal of Forensic Medicine and Pathology* 1991;12(1):27–32.

8. Smialek J. E., Smialek P. Z., Spitz W. U. Accidental bed deaths in infants due to unsafe sleeping situations. *Clinical Pediatrics (Philadelphia)* 1977;16(11):1031–1036.

9. Nakamura S., Wind M., Danello M. A. Review of hazards associated with children placed in adult beds. *Archives of Pediatrics and Adolescent Medicine* 1999;153(10):1019–1023.

10. Blair P. S. et al. Babies sleeping with parents: Care-control study of factors influencing the risk of the sudden infant death syndrome. *British Medical Journal*;319(7223):1457–1462 (December 4, 1999).

11. Matthews H. B., Eustis S. L., Haseman J. Toxicity and carcinogenicity of chronic exposure to tris(2-chloroethyl)phosphate. *Fundamental and Applied Toxicology* 1993;20(4):477–485.

12. Cunningham M. L., Elwell M. R., Matthews H. B. Site-specific cell proliferation in renal tubular cells by the renal tubular carcinogen tris(2,3-dibromopropyl)phosphate. *Environmental Health Perspectives* 1993;101 Suppl 5:253–257.

13. Scragg R. K., Mitchell E. A. Side sleeping position and bed sharing in the sudden infant death syndrome. *Annals of Medicine* 1998; 30(4):345–349.

Chapter 5

1. Wirz-Justice A. et al. "Natural" light treatment of seasonal affective disorder. *Journal of Affective Disorders*;37(2–3):109–120 (April 12, 1996).

2. Perez Navero J. L. et al. [Effects of competitive physical exercise on neuroendocrine response and interleukin-6 liberation in children.] *Anales Españoles de Pediatría* 1999;51(3):267–272.

3. Buxton O. M., L'Hermite-Baleriaux M., Hirschfeld U., Cauter E.

Acute and delayed effects of exercise on human melatonin secretion. *Journal of Biological Rhythms* 1997;12(6):568–574.

4. Buxton O. M. et al. Roles of intensity and duration of nocturnal exercise in causing phase delays of human circadian rhythms. *Americal Journal of Physiology* 1997;273(3 Pt 1):E536–542.

5. Van Reeth O. et al. Nocturnal exercise phase delays circadian rhythms of melatonin and thyrotropin secretion in normal men. *American Journal of Physiology* 1994;266(6 Pt 1):E964–974.

6. Wetterberg L. Melatonin and clinical application. *Reproduction, Nutrition, Development* 1999;39(3):367–382.

7. Skene D. J., Lockley S. W., Thapan K., Arendt J. Effects of light on human circadian rhythms. *Reproduction, Nutrition, Development* 1999;39(3):295–304.

8. Park S. J., Tokura H. Bright light exposure during the daytime affects circadian rhythms of urinary melatonin and salivary immunoglobulin A. *Chronobiology International* 1999;16(3):359–371.

9. Wehr T. A. Seasonal vulnerability to depression. Implications for etiology and treatment. *Encephale* 1992;18 Spec No 4:479–483.

10. Lansdowne A. T., Provost S. C. Vitamin D3 enhances mood in healthy subjects during winter. *Psychopharmacology (Berlin)* 1998; 135(4):319–323.

11. Lam R. W., Buchanan A., Mador J. A., Corral M. R., Remick R. A. The effects of ultraviolet-A wavelengths in light therapy for seasonal depression. *Journal of Affective Disorders* 1992;24(4):237–243.

12. Lam R. W., Buchanan A., Clark C. M., Remick R. A. Ultraviolet versus non-ultraviolet light therapy for seasonal affective disorder. *Journal of Clinical Psychiatry* 1991;52(5):213–216.

13. Painter W. Sunshine and turnip greens. Medication is not always the best cure for depression. *Contemporary Longterm Care* 1999; 22(3):72–73.

14. Dralle D., Bodeker R. H. Serum magnesium level and sleep behavior of newborn infants. *European Journal of Pediatrics* 1980;134(3): 239–243.

Chapter 6

1. Bass H. N. "Bubble bath" as an irritant to the urinary tract of children. *Clinical Pediatrics (Philadelphia)* 1968;7:174.

2. Mueller E. R., Steinhardt G, Naseer S. The incidence of genito-urinary abnormalities in circumcised and uncircumcised boys presenting with an initial urinary tract infection by 6 months of age. *Pediatrics* 1997;100 Suppl 3:580.

3. Winberg J., Gothefors L., Bollgren I., Herthelius M. The prepuce: A mistake of nature? *Lancet* 1989;1(8638):598–599.

4. Crain-Thoreson C., Dale P. S. Do early talkers become early readers? Linguistic precocity, preschool language, and emergent literacy. *Developmental Psychology* 1992;28(3):421–429.

5. Kliewer, Gary. The Mozart Effect. *New Scientist*;164(2211):35–37 (November 6, 1999).

6. Polan H. J., Ward M. J. Role of the mother's touch in failure to thrive: A preliminary investigation. *Journal of the American Academy of Child and Adolescent Psychiatry* 1994;33(8):1098–1105 (October).

7. Hamelin K., Ramachandran C. Kangaroo care. *Canadian Nurse* 1993;89(6):15–17.

8. Ludington-Hoe S. M., Swinth J. Y. Developmental aspects of kangaroo care. *Journal of Obstetric, Gynecologic, and Neonatal Nursing* 1996;25(8):691–703.

9. Ludington-Hoe S. M. et al. Birth-related fatigue in 34–36-week preterm neonates: Rapid recovery with very early kangaroo (skin-to-skin) care. *Journal of Obstetric, Gynecologic, and Neonatal Nursing* 1999;28(1):94–103.

10. Charpak N., Ruiz-Pelaez J. G., Figueroa de C-Z, Charpak Y. Kangaroo mother versus traditional care for newborn infants </=2000 grams: A randomized, controlled trial. *Pediatrics* 1997; 100(4):682–688.

11. Tessier R. et al. Kangaroo mother care and the bonding hypothesis. *Pediatrics* 1998;102(2):e17.

12. Anderson G. C. Current knowledge about skin-to-skin (kangaroo) care for preterm infants. *Journal of Perinatology* 1991;11(3): 216–226.

Chapter 7

1. Schachter F. F., Fuchs M. L., Bijur P. E., Stone R. K. Cosleeping and sleep problems in Hispanic-American urban young children. *Pediatrics* 1989;84(3):522–530.
2. Klonoff-Cohen H., Edelstein S. L. Bed sharing and the sudden infant death syndrome. *British Medical Journal* 1995;311(7015): 1269–1272 (November 11, 1995).
3. Scragg R. K. et al. Infant room-sharing and prone sleep position in sudden infant death syndrome. New Zealand Cot Death Study Group. *Lancet*;347(8993):7–12 (January 6, 1996).
4. Mosko S., Richard C., McKenna J. Infant arousals during mother-infant bed sharing: Implications for infant sleep and sudden infant death syndrome research. *Pediatrics* 1997;100(5):841–849.
5. Scragg R. K. et al. Infant room-sharing and prone sleep position in sudden infant death syndrome. New Zealand Cot Death Study Group. *Lancet*;347(8993):7–12 (January 6, 1996).
6. See: McKenna J. J. Cultural influences on infant and childhood sleep biology, and the science that studies it: Toward a more inclusive paradigm. In: Loughlin J., Marcus C., Carroll J., eds. *Sleep in Development and Pediatrics.* New York: Marcel Dakker, 1999. [in press]
7. Billingham R. E., Zentall S. Co-sleeping: Gender differences in college students' retrospective reports of sleeping with parents during childhood. *Psychological Reports* 1996;79(3 Pt 2): 1423–1426.
8. For more information on circumcision, see the following books: Denniston G. C., F. M. Hodges, M. F. Milos, eds. *Male and Female Circumcision: Medical, Ethical, and Legal Issues in Pediatric Practice.* New York: Kluwer Academic/Plenum Press, 1999.

Denniston G. C., M. F. Milos, eds. *Sexual Mutilations: A Human Tragedy*. New York: Plenum Press, 1997.

Ritter, Thomas, and George C. Denniston. *Say No to Circumcision* 2d ed. Aptos: Hourglass, 1996.

O'Mara, Peggy, ed. *Circumcision: The Rest of the Story*. Santa Fe: Mothering, 1993.

Goldman, Ronald. *Circumcision: The Hidden Trauma*. Boston: Vanguard, 1996.

Goldman, Ronald. *Questioning Circumcision: A Jewish Perspective*. Boston: Vanguard, 1998.

Boyd, Billy Ray. *Circumcision Exposed: Rethinking a Medical and Cultural Tradition*. Freedom, Calif.: The Crossing Press, 1998.

The following websites are also useful:

http://www.cirp.org/

http://www.infocirc.org/index-e.htm

http://www.nocirc.org/

9. Goode, Erica. "Baby in Parent's Bed in Danger? U.S. Says Yes, but Others Demur." *New York Times* (September 30, 1999).

10. Cited in: Radice, Sophie. If you sleep with your baby, here's a wake-up call. *Guardian*, no. 47,622 (Wednesday, October 6, 1999): G2:9.

11. Nakamura S., Wind M., Danello M. A. Review of hazards associated with children placed in adult beds. *Archives of Pediatrics and Adolescent Medicine* 1999;153(10):1019–1023.

12. Gilbert-Barness E. et al. Hazards of mattresses, beds and bedding in deaths of infants. *American Journal of Forensic Medicine and Pathology* 1991;12(1):27–32.

13. Byard R. W., Beal S., Bourne A. J. Potentially dangerous sleeping environments and accidental asphyxia in infancy and early childhood. *Archives of Disease in Childhood* 1994;71(6):497–500.

14. Scragg R. K., Mitchell E. A. Side sleeping position and bed sharing in the sudden infant death syndrome. *Annals of Medicine* 1998; 30(4):345–349.

15. Blair P. S. et al. Babies sleeping with parents: Case-control study of factors influencing the risk of the sudden infant death syndrome. *British Journal of Urology*;319(7223):1457–1462 (December 4, 1999).

16. Mitchell E. A. et al. Risk factors for sudden infant death syndrome following the prevention campaign in New Zealand: A prospective study. *Pediatrics* 1997;100(5):835–840.

17. Brooke H., Gibson A., Tappin D., Brown H. Case-control study of sudden infant death syndrome in Scotland, 1992–5. *British Medical Journal*;314(7093):1516–1520 (May 24, 1997).

18. Fleming P. J. et al. Environment of infants during sleep and risk of the sudden infant death syndrome: Results of 1993–5 case-control study for confidential inquiry into stillbirths and deaths in infancy. Confidential Enquiry into Stillbirths and Deaths Regional Coordinators and Researchers. *British Medical Journal*;313(7051):191–195 (July 27, 1996).

19. Richard C. A. Increased infant axillary temperatures in non-REM sleep during mother-infant bed-sharing. *Early Human Development* 1999;55(2):103–111.

20. Tuffnel C. S., Petersen S. A., Wailoo M. P. Higher rectal temperatures in co-sleeping infants. *Archives of Disease in Childhood* 1996; 75(3):249–250.

21. Petersen S. A., Wailoo M. P. Interactions between infant care practices and physiological development in Asian infants. *Early Human Development*;38(3):181–186 (September 15, 1994).

22. Richard C. A., Mosko S. S., McKenna J. J. Apnea and periodic breathing in bed-sharing and solitary sleeping infants. *Journal of Applied Physiology* 1998;84(4):1374–1380.

23. Mosko S., Richard C., McKenna J. Maternal sleep and arousals during bedsharing with infants. *Sleep* 1997;20(2):142–150.

24. Mosko S., Richard C., McKenna J., Drummond S. Infants sleep architecture during bedsharing and possible implications for SIDS. *Sleep* 1996;19(9):677–684.

25. McKenna J. J., Mosko S. S. Sleep and arousal, synchrony and independence, among mothers and infants sleeping apart and together (same bed): An experiment in evolutionary medicine. *Acta Paediatrica Supplement* 1994;397:94–102.

26. Mosko S., McKenna J., Dickel M., Hunt L. Parent-infant co-sleeping: The appropriate context for the study of infant sleep and implications for sudden infant death syndrome (SIDS) research. *Journal of Behavioral Medicine* 1993;16(6):589–610.

27. McKenna J. J., Mosko S., Dungy C., McAninch J. Sleep and arousal patterns of co-sleeping human mother/infant pairs: A preliminary physiological study with implications for the study of sudden infant death syndrome (SIDS). *American Journal of Physical Anthropology* 1990;83(3):331–347.

28. McKenna J. J., Mosko S. S., Richard C. A. Bedsharing promotes breastfeeding. *Pediatrics* 1997;100(2 Pt 1):214–219.

29. McKenna J. et al. Experimental studies of infant-parent co-sleeping: Mutual physiological and behavioral influences and their relevance to SIDS (sudden infant death syndrome). *Early Human Development*;38(3):187–201 (September 15, 1994).

30. Richard C., Mosko S., McKenna J., Drummond S. Sleeping position, orientation, and proximity in bedsharing infants and mothers. *Sleep* 1996;19(9):685–690.

31. Billingham R. E., Zentall S. Co-sleeping: Gender differences in college students' restrospective reports of sleeping with parents during childhood. *Psychological Reports* 1996;79(3 Pt 2): 1423–1426.

32. Hernandez J. T. Substance abuse among sexually abused adolescents and their families. *Journal of Adolescent Health* 1992;13(8): 658–662.

33. Yellowleess P. M., Kaushik A. V. The Broken Hill Psychopathology Project. *Australian and New Zealand Journal of Psychiatry* 1992; 26(2):197–207.

34. Gordon M. The family environment of sexual abuse: A comparison of natal and stepfather abuse. *Child Abuse & Neglect* 1989;13(1): 121–130.

35. Famularo R., Stone K., Barnum R., Wharton R. Alcoholism and severe child maltreatment. *American Journal of Orthopsychiatry* 1986; 56(3):481–485.

36. Kirkland K. D., Bauer C. A. MMPI traits of incestuous fathers. *Journal of Clinical Psychology* 1982;38(3):645–649.

Index